ALSO BY BRENT HAROLD

The Novel and Human Problems
Bodywork
Wellfleet and the World

OWNING THE SIERRA NEVADA

*the short history
of a long infatuation*

BRENT HAROLD

KINNACUM PRESS
Wellfleet Massachusetts

Published in 2006 in the United States by:

Kinnacum Press
P.O. Box 1683
Wellfleet, MA 02667
email: Kinnacum@capecod.net

Printed in the United States

Library of Congress Control Number: 2006900219
ISBN 10: 0-9655598-2-3
ISBN 13: 978-0-9655598-2-9

for Ben, who knows a thing or two about western mountains, including how to bust a fire the old-fashioned way;

Burt Blum, loyal keeper of our land;

Art Poulin, who embodies the spirit of the old Coldstream and built a cool cabin which does the same;

and of course Hoss, trailmate.

For most of us, our romantic fate, the account of our romantic life, is a central, recurrent narrative within the stories we tell others about ourselves and the stories we tell ourselves about ourselves. . . .

—Stephen A. Mitchell, *Can Love Last?*

Contents

OWNING
THE
SIERRA NEVADA

Favoring my sore foot, I manage to hop a couple of rocks across the near creek, which at this time of year doesn't have much of a flow, clamber on all fours up the mossy bank and hobble over in the direction of the far creek. See what we can do about finding one of those old boards to make a camp bench. Ben romps ahead. The smell of the pine needles baking in the noon sun is strong. Good to be here smelling it, to be moving, however cautiously, up the open slope. The sweet smell of the manzanita blossoms kicks in. Catch a glimpse of the ridge over my right shoulder. "Hey, Ben, see the patch of snow up there? That never melts. Like a mini-glacier." Not as impressed as he might be.

Through a grove of spaced pines, dappled sun. Farther than I remember it over to the other creek. Especially with a sore ankle. Ah, here we go. Full of rushing water, as always. A chaos of downed tree trunks. And yet familiar. Still a pool down there, a bit of waterfall over that hunk of tree jammed athwart the main flow. Could that be the same one from almost 30 years ago? You'd think the violence of the spring floods, the unleashing of the meltoff from the deep winter snows, would transform this place unrecognizably every year.

"That's where we always thought we would build a dam to make a swimming hole," I tell Ben. "And up there"—just upstream of us the land begins its rise up to the ridge, creating a gorge with steep walls of loose dirt and rock—"we were going to build a bridge of some sort, maybe a rope bridge." I like explaining this history to him, but you never can tell if he is really taking it in.

The ankle feels looser with the exercise and I surprise myself by my competence in skidding down the bank, making it from rock to rock across the fast-flowing water to the old sluice, still visible through the undergrowth on the far bank. Pretty quickly I locate a 2-by-12 board—weathered and beat-up of course but only a little decayed at one end, despite sitting exposed for all these years. Still pink when you scratch through the soft, grey surface. "Ben, check this out—this is redwood. Amazing stuff. Could be a hundred years old."

Ben takes off a sneaker, sticks his foot in the water, jerks it right out again. Whoa! So much for that refreshing dip he was contemplating. I point up to the ridge: "That's where this water is coming from; this was snow only a short time ago."

There are at least eight to ten good feet in this plank. It may be the last decent one we will get from the old sluice. I wrestle it loose, upend it, let it fall across rocks, making a bridge to re-cross the creek. Then, Ben on one end and I on the other, we drag the board back up the bank and retrace our steps to the campsite, stopping a couple of times to pocket rusty spikes that fall out of the board. They may come in handy for the project. My foot feeling looser and more normal by the minute.

PART
ONE

'68: A Good Idea At the Time

^ ^ ^

Once upon a time, in another world, ten friends bought a piece of land together. It was 1968. We were youngish academics and professionals living in an area south of San Francisco centered around Stanford University in Palo Alto. The land we bought was a piece of that Shangri-La, the Sierra Nevada.

I had been making my way for the better part of that watershed decade through the English Department's degree program, with many a detour from the academic straight-and-narrow. In no particular hurry to become a professional grownup I had, just by being part of the cultural mix of those pre-Silicon Valley days, gotten to witness what seemed to the impressionable youth that I was amazing, new and emblematic things. There was the evening at Kepler's bookstore hangout when Joan Baez lit a small cigar with a flaming five dollar bill. (More like $50, corrected for inflation, but the gesture was not as radical as it seems; home in the first flush of success in the East, she could afford it.) There was Kesey, returned from Mexico, showing off the U.S. flag enameled on a front tooth. I was mostly impressed by his willingness to mess up his smile to make an ironic political statement. Too timid to go myself, I lapped up Frank Jones' stories of Sexual Freedom League parties. This was before he discovered that he was the only avatar of God in 2000 years and became, at first as Da Free John, more recently as Adi Da, the focus of a worldwide religion. Like a lot of other folks, I was sucked into the vortex of the famous Prankster-Hell's Angel party across the hills in La Honda by rumors of the apocalyptic gang bang, among other excesses chronicled in Tom Wolfe's *The Electric Kool-Aid Acid Test*. I was there in the cottage up the row from mine at Homer Lane the moment when Richard Alpert in his pre-Ram Dass days—or was it Leary?—declared that the only task remaining for the human race was to figure out how to "stay high all the time."

More comfortable as an observer than a participant in a lot of these highlights, I nevertheless thoroughly bought into the spirit of it. It felt, as many have said of the heady atmosphere of those days in that place, as if "we" were mid-wifing a New Age.

Our communal land purchase late in the fast-morphing decade, didn't at the time seem especially cutting edge or part of a new world. Unlike the most committed citizens of the counter-culture (as it had yet to be called), we were keeping our day jobs. Even I had gotten my act together, passed the dreaded exams, was steaming ahead on the dissertation and had recently landed an academic appointment out there in the real professional world. Nevertheless, the cultural phenomenon that brought us together was a 'sixties phenomenon, an "encounter group" that met for six to eight hours every other Saturday. An encounter group was a radical sort of psychotherapy that had, in its own view of itself, broken free of the traditional notion of therapy as professional help for neurotic, troubled people. We thought of ourselves less as patients than as a liberated, Aquarian age elite engaging in a high-consciousness version of traditional coupling and families, with an emphasis on intent listening, heartfelt advice and frequent hugs. In its open-ended structure and lack of clear professional boundaries—we thought of our therapist and he may well have thought of himself more as one of us than standing outside as a detached professional—our group was less psychotherapy than

utopian community. It was this community that gener-
ated the impulse to buy communal land.

So: nothing so radical as destroying currency or de-
facing a tooth to make a point, but buying property
outside the context of marriage or business, merely to
celebrate friendship, was in its own way a typical moment in that utopian era.

~

A careless, revisionist history of mid- to southern Bay
Area would probably see our group as marginal characters in an early chapter of what turned out to be the
big story of our time, the personal computer revolution. We would have resisted any such interpretation.
Our area was not to be known as Silicon Valley for
a few years and although even then technology companies like H-P and SRI might have been the eco-
nomic bedrock of the area, most of us were marching
to a different drummer. A number of people in the
encounter group worked in technology but careers as
such were treated by us as rumors of little interest
compared with participation in our New Age community. It was only decades later, in a display at the Boston Science Museum on revered fathers of the computer revolution, that I recognized the photo of Doug
Englebart and read that during the time I knew him
in the encounter group he was well along in the work

that would make him famous as the inventor of the mouse and other key aspects of the personal computer. As far as most of us were concerned at the time he was just an older-than-average member of the group with an issue around delegating authority.

Somewhat fewer than half the members of the encounter group ended up being land partners. Of those Harlan, Burt and Bill had technology jobs. Dave, Jim, Elaine, and I were in the final stages of getting our PhDs in English at Stanford. Stephan's degree was in economics. Helen was an artist and mother. Jan, a former schoolteacher, was headed for a classic dropout year as a ski bum. Most of us were expatriates from the East, remote from our communities of origin and happy to be so. All of us were unmarried at the time, although most of us had been married. Only two of those early, failed marriages had produced children.

The proximate cause of the urge to buy communal land was the imminent departure of the five academics for first teaching jobs in the East. Within a few months the realities of the job market would be breaking up that old gang of ours, as the old song went. Owning land in common would be an expression of commitment to the future of our friendship, both a legal bond and a physical venue for reunion now that we would no longer share the Bay Area or the encounter group.

The communal impulse was the ostensible motivation for buying the land, but for me there was an ulterior motive: simply wanting to possess a piece of the West. However it was for the other land partners from the East, and most were, my decision to take a job back East created the possibility of tragic conflict. I had made the trek all the way to California to go to graduate school in large part because of the influence of Kerouac's *On the Road*, with its depiction of a still wild West, although with the usual meaning of "wild" tweaked, in the beatnik use of this term, to mean edgy, far-out. Graduate school in English is a mild-mannered occupation but the West of Kerouac—and in the culture in general—was something else again: a place of possibility, inspiring utopian dreams; an empty place (in the racist myth) where you go to create a new life out of raw material, in the process remaking yourself.

Early in my eight years of drifting through graduate school I had learned to refer to my coast of origin in the California fashion as "back East," with its implicit contrast with the more adventurous-sounding "out West"—as in going West, young man, and either making a go of it or returning, with a hint of retreat. Leaving to take that job back East felt like abandoning what I had come to see as my real home. Buying a piece of the mythic terrain was a way of hedging my bets.

Envisioning much more than a yearly camporee with old friends, I didn't, as unrealistic as it may seem, see myself as moving back East. The great thing about an academic schedule was the large chunks of the year left free of teaching and other strictly scheduled activity. The way I had it figured, the long academic summer, three and a half months, plus several weeks off around the Christmas holidays, would make possible close to a halftime life in California. At the farthest stretch of my fantasy, I would be, in essence, commuting to the job in the East from my real life in the West, whose centerpiece would henceforth be the Sierra land.

~

But why the Sierra? Why not something in Palo Alto, the home turf? Or over the hills on the coast, where I had in fact lived communally for a year on the edge of the Pacific? Again, I won't presume to speak for the others, although several of us had skied together in the Sierra. For me, by 1968, the mountains were radiant with association and meaning. In the earliest 'sixties I had made several trips to Yosemite, John Muir's playground, which was much less crowded in those years. (The last visit I made, in the early 80s, they had begun to control crowding by requiring registration and assigning you to a block on a grid—something of a damper on one's romancing of the high country.)

A few years into grad school, sitting for hours in the library and performing other acts of the scholarly life were losing out in the competition with other of life's possibilities for a young man. Feeling more and more a citizen of the Stanford ambience than an actual Stanford student, I dropped out, as Leary had not quite gotten around to legitimating it. At about the same time I also dropped out of what was left of my youthful marriage. As a sort of emancipation proclamation I packed some books and writing paper into my VW bug and headed up to the Gold Lake-Sierra Buttes high country for what has turned out the only solo backpacking trip of my life. I walked a few miles into a small lake, rolled out my spartan ensolite pad and sleeping bag on smooth granite and slept under the stars with only the entire universe for company. It was something like what came to be known as a vision quest I was after—some deeper knowledge of myself from this glorious setting. I was not entirely without distraction, however, as I had packed a Jane Austen novel along and read myself to sleep with it. My choice of literary companion (instead, say, of Gary Snyder or a haiku poet) would seem to be strange, even contradictory; Jane would have found the wilderness excessive and tacky, if not threatening, and my transcendental purpose as incompatible with her world as a bull in a china closet. But I was quite conscious of the comfort of her domestic drama as a hedge against the All there at 7000 feet. And, separated from my wife, there was, in addition to the spiritual ambitions inspired by the scenery, the more mundane hope that a female soulmate on her own similar quest would materialize out of the emptiness. But Jane was my only female company on that adventure.

Even without actual sex, the Sierra itself was sexy terrain. On one impromptu trip, a friend and I are buying some supplies from what was called in those days the health food store when we meet a girl who decides then and there to join us—sure, why not, let's go. She has no sleeping bag, only the clothes she is wearing, so it seems likely, since my friend is married, and I recently separated, that she is destined for my sleeping bag, which adds zest to the adventure. Of the girl I have only a vague recollection, mostly the discomfort of trying to stay warm at 8000 feet in Tuolomne Meadows in a single bag which had to be unzipped to accommodate us both. What stands out when I think of that trip is the sexiness simply of being in the high Sierra: smooth, clean rock, pure water, eternal snow, and the huge bowl of dark blue sky. I used the word purity a lot in those days for the mountain experience. Sexy purity? Ascetic sensuousness? They sound like oxymorons;

but I didn't experience it that way. That largely tree-less, rockbound landscape was sexy in the sense of making one feel exposed—to an intimate connection with the cosmos; or with something. ('Scuse me while I kiss the sky.) Dropped out of key human relationships in my life, I felt in the mountains more connected to life in general.

On another trip I am sitting crosslegged on a boulder at 10,000 feet, breathing deeply of the sweet, thin air, composing a haiku-like poem to a Bay Area girlfriend in which I somehow manage in my lust to compare the bare beauty of the granite vistas about me, the exposed ribs of the Sierra, with the bare beauty of her fine-boned body. The relationship with this woman has not been going my way and I am hopeful that by beaming this imagery at her across the intervening valley miles I can do my cause some good.

All of this, in addition to my communal urges, was in my desire to own land in the mountains.

~

Scouting parties of the most motivated of us made forays in the summer of '68 across California's Central Valley into the foothills and mountains, eventually settling on 20 acres of high Sierra just over Donner pass, a few miles from Donner Lake and Truckee. In those days $1000 per acre didn't seem a particularly good deal for raw, relatively inaccessible land. On the other hand, it seemed miraculous to me that we could actually possess this piece of genuine High Sierra, all the glories one would think could be owned, only distantly, as citizens "own" our national parks. Buying it communally made it relatively painless despite my graduate student poverty. It was my first purchase of real estate. We had a lawyer draw up and we all signed a "Joint Venture Agreement" formalizing our sentimental attachment.

I flew back East to take my job late in the summer of 1968, not long after our first time camping on The Land (as we called it from the start, as if it were the only land). The plane's flight path took us, as it happened, right over it; I recognized it from my study of the topographical map of the area by its proximity to a prominent hairpin turn in the railroad tracks. I felt both real grief over leaving it behind and determination to return the following summer.

A number of us did indeed converge on The Land early the following summer for a big reunion. Some of us made more visits that summer. We chose tentative sites for individual cabins for sleep and study and talked at night around the campfire about the large building we would be constructing for communal eating and socializing. We went so far as to imagine ourselves, the academics among us at any rate, as Coldstream Summer Institute (or something of the sort) which would host conferences on advanced topics. But some partners didn't come that first year, some came only that year, and one or two, I believe, have, despite their financial investment, never visited the place. I doubt that communal thoughts were entertained by any of us after the first year or two.

In fact, only Burt and I of the original partners have gone there with any regularity and my own record is hardly one of constancy. Of the 36 years of our ownership, my total time there amounts to between three and four months. And yet that attenuated physical presence belies the importance of this place in my life.

The communal impulse died aborning; but we didn't sell the land, in part because it didn't seem worth enough to go to the trouble to sell it. Perhaps more of us than just I felt they could afford to keep it to fantasize about. Our twenty acres sat there, untouched by our original designs on it, raw material for romancing for those so inclined.

All That Real Property

∧　　∧　　∧

Our piece of the Sierra is legally defined as follows
in the deed: "all that real property situate in the un-
incorporated area of County of Placer, State of California, described as follows· The South one-half of
the Southeast one-quarter of the Southeast quarter of
Section 26. . . ." Using that description, our piece is
easily identifiable on a U. S. Geological Survey topographical map as a rectangle in the lower right corner
of Section 26, twice as wide in the East-West direction
as in the North-South direction. That same information
is encountered on a walk up the Tinker Knob road as
you cross our southern boundary. There, nailed to a
tree by the USGS people is a dented, yellow metal card
with a tic, tac, toe of square mile sections on which

that precise point where you stand looking at the card
is marked with a tack with a notation of the distance
from that point to the southeast corner of Section 26. It
is a satisfying congruence of the abstract and concrete:
your land as part of the official grid which parcels up
the whole country, with its correspondence to actual
lines of latitude and longitude that parcel up the whole
globe.

Surrounded for the most part by the huge Tahoe National Forest, our land is situated at the end of the Coldstream Valley (occasionally called on maps Coldstream
Canyon, which has a nice western sound to it), which
drains a portion of the eastern slope of the main ridge
of the Sierra, about ten miles northwest of Lake Tahoe, that big, deep high mountain lake which straddles
the California/Nevada border. Looking toward civilization out the valley to the northeast is Donner Lake,
the forced winter residence of the unfortunate pioneer
party of that name, and a bit farther, the town with the
colorful (if inelegant) name of Truckee.

It is on our acreage that the valley divides into two
watersheds, one flowing down from Mt. Lincoln and
the other from the curiously named Tinker Knob, which
is less a discrete peak than a bump on the spine of the
mountain range. At some point I was under the impres-
sion that a tinker's knob was part of the toolkit of an

old-fashioned, itinerant mender of household utensils. But a local history says the name does honor to the prominent nose of J.A. Tinker, a "hard driving, wild-drinking mountain teamster" (Joanne Meschery, *Truckee: An Illustrated History of the Town and its Surroundings*). I would like to give this account my vote on the basis of color alone, but the fact is the topographical feature in question looks more like a knob than a nose; I don't know why they wouldn't have called it Tinker's Nose if that's what they meant.

Both Tinker Knob and Mt. Lincoln are close to 9000' in elevation, which is as high as the Sierra get this far north. About one hundred miles to the south as the eagle flies are the 12000' peaks of John Muir's Yosemite and a like distance beyond that the over 14000' mountains of King's Canyon and Sequoia parks. Within fifty miles or so to the north of us the Sierra peters out altogether. From the top of Tinker Knob on a typically clear day you can see all the way the roughly 100 miles to Lassen Peak, the southernmost outpost of the Cascade Range.

If our peaks are more modest than those to the south they are thousands of feet higher than the tallest peaks of the Appalachian chain in the East. Even more impressive than that to an easterner is the fact that the elevation of our property on the valley floor, at 6200', is exactly the height of New Hampshire's Mt. Washington, the tallest mountain in the northeast.

~

The summer of '69 I spent a number of hours making a map of our place, first getting clear about its shape from the topo map and deed description, then pacing off the bounds, as best I could determine them, and distances from the bounds to big rocks and other landmarks. The pacing was often difficult, involving a lot of tromping through stiff brush, and there was a certain amount of guesswork and estimating. I discovered it isn't easy getting a sense from the ground of even such modest acreage as ours and could sympathize with the makers of all the crude maps of various parts of the world in the Age of Exploration, as they called it in grade school. Once that summer Harlan, who had a pilot's license, flew me over Coldstream and from what I could see from a few hundred feet up, my map had it basically right; and in any case I assume that, despite its shortcomings, this is still the most detailed map in existence of this particular 20 acre portion of the world's surface. We had already come up with names to use on the map: Helen had both a boulder and a meadow named after her. There was Dave's Rock, the Fourth of July Camp, named for the date of the reunion camporee; and Beaver Totem—

named for the anonymous rodent who chewed a tall stump in a corkscrew as the snow level in some long past spring melted from six feet.

The two streams do much to define our property. The one called Cold Creek, which, since the valley is named after it, would seem to indicate the dominant branch, is actually the tamer of the two. It flows through more accessible meadows and is therefore where we established our main campsite. There are signs that in winter or spring runoff it gets wild enough, but in the summer it is sedate and in August disappears underground for stretches. Often it seems dry in the morning, but by mid afternoon is flowing again. The far creek, the South Fork, originating in the snow fields below Tinker Knob, is always full, always rushing and has cut a steep ravine which ends just over our southern boundary (partway up to Tinker it makes an impressive waterfall of 30 to 40 feet).

The other main organizing features of our corner of the Sierra are two rough, dirt roads basically following the two streams up toward the respective peaks. The one heading up toward Tinker Knob, but turning into trail less than halfway, begins to rise on our property. The other one, which cuts through a corner of our land on its way up to Mt. Lincoln is, according to posted signs along the way, the Emigrant Trail, one of the routes pioneered by later wagon trains seeking to avoid the fate of the Donner Party in 1846 by using an easier pass through the mountains than the formidable stone wall looming over Donner Lake.

Our proximity to the Horseshoe Bend of the Southern Pacific railroad is another distinctive feature that relates our acres to the world. It is actually more a hairpin than a horseshoe, when you look at it on the topo map: four miles out our valley toward us from Truckee, making what for a railroad seems a very sharp bend, about three-quarters of a mile from us, and four miles back again up the southeast slope of Schallenberger Ridge toward Donner Lake, the whole purpose being to gain elevation for the climb over Donner Pass.

The dirt road out our valley runs between the sides of the hairpin and intersects the railroad at the sharp bend. One problem with this is that unless the railroad company puts a "crossing" in the form of a bed of railroad ties installed between the tracks—only, as far as I can tell, at the behest of a lumber company—most cars and trucks can't get across. Until recently this has meant parking on the Truckee side of the railroad and doing a bit of backpacking that one would be just as happy to avoid: one or more trips with heavily laden pack, pots and pans and camp chairs tied on and banging about; a lumpish, ice-filled cooler awkwardly slung between two people, banging one's legs.

Communing

∧ ∧ ∧

One of the places we had looked at land to buy was the vicinity of the South Fork of the Yuba River where it is crossed by Route 49 in the foothills a few miles north of Nevada City. This spot was a favorite of several of the land partners and, even after we bought the Coldstream land, visits from the Bay Area, where I was based the summer of '69, usually included a detour from the Interstate beeline up 49 to the Yuba. In the late 'sixties Nevada City was not the gentrified destination of interest in itself it was to become; it was only the town you went through on the way to the Yuba. Several features combine to make that particular spot on the river the Mother of All Swimming Holes: a steep gorge, the contrast between hot, dry air and deep pools of cool but swimmable water, snowmelt from the high mountains warmed by this point in its journey to the valley to a perfectly refreshing temperature. Most distinctive of all are the boulders filling the bottom of the gorge, smoothed and rounded and bleached by eons of flooding into sensuous, fantastic shapes, some suggestive of Henry Moore sculptures. Most are as softly receptive to the lounging human form as stone gets.

The pools upstream from the bridge crossing, with its more accessible swimming, were reachable in those days only by precarious paths barely scratched by usage into the precipitous, dusty sides of the gorge. Their relative remoteness made them favorites for an increasing number of pilgrims for nude swimming and sunbathing. I was an habitue of several summers' standing when I took a girlfriend from the East there. Arriving upstream at our usual pool, it became clear that nudity was the order of the day. Jane, not normally shy, hesitated. Are you sure it's OK? she asked. The implication was that, unleashed on an unsuspecting world, her ample charms might trigger chaos. An understandable concern, I reassured her, but no worries in this ultimate cool scene.

And it was a cool scene. In a world of burgeoning war in Vietnam, escalating protest at home, and hot weather riots in cities, the Yuba was a utopian oasis of unarmed and undefended strangers co-existing in sensual pleasure in this remarkable place. Some, perhaps part of the hippie exodus from the cities, had begun calling this stretch of the river home, constructing crude hovels of driftwood, living from jars of beans, rice, and other virtuous fare; lean, brown, spiritual river people smoking pot the whole day long. Simply that there was such a place—virtually unknown except to locals until the '60s, not prevented by private property, and self-regulating—seemed a little piece of paradise leftover.

Inevitably, presumably necessarily, 20 years after our heyday, this place on the Yuba was simultaneously honored and officially pronounced unable to fend for itself by being designated a state park. At the stroke of a pen the old, unregulated swimmin' hole was killed off and declared a public recreational resource. The precarious trails upstream have been made safer for the visiting public by strategically placed footbridges and steps. The original Route 49 bridge, replaced by a more efficient and more perfunctory bridge a short distance downstream, has been retired as part of the park itself, a relic of the old days.

~

We would arrive at the Yuba midday and spend the afternoon alternately immersing and baking ourselves, with the occasional foray upstream, bounding naked from rock to rock. As shadows began to fill the bottom of the gorge, we would hike out, stop to pick up cheap steak and wine and other supplies at the Bonanza Market in Nevada City then head on up the 60 miles or so and 5000 vertical feet to the refreshingly alpine world of Coldstream. Arriving at dusk just as the mosquitoes began to swarm, we pulled on long pants and sweatshirts or jackets over bodies still warm from the hours at the Yuba. Chilly air begins to settle into our valley as evening comes on, making welcome both fire and heavier clothing and eventually discouraging the mosquitoes. The temperatures of Coldstream, at an elevation of over 6000 feet, drop quickly from an afternoon high in the 80s through the 60s and 50s as one prepares dinner, heading down for early morning temperatures often in the 30s and occasionally into the 20s, as evidenced by ice in dishes left out the night before. That's as much as an 80 degree drop from the typical heat of the desert or Central Valley.

After the inevitable confusions of cooking and eating in the dying light, we would settle in around the fire for communing on into the night, passing a gallon jug of the cheapest wine and maybe smoking some pot. Sometimes, in a lull in the talk, we would hear a faroff train and some of us would jump up and race it to the crossing, stand and watch its immensity materialize out of the dark, the headlight swinging around until it shone right at us, having to trust that it would stay on the tracks which, blinded by the light, we could not see but knew to curve in front of us.

Fire-making is always a pleasure. There is plenty of dry, bleached wood to be found nearby, unlike the East, where most camping grounds are picked over and any firewood found likely to be damp from a recent rain. In five minutes you have sticks for a cooking fire and thicker branches for the sitting-around stage of the evening; one match and a piece of balled up newspaper and presto, a relatively smokeless fire. Hardly a test of your firebuilding skills.

As the years passed the wine came in smaller bottles, was more likely to be sipped than gulped; and the late evening encounter with the train was less and less tempting. But sitting around the fire is what the day always boils down to, the world narrowed to a particular glowing log or branch and the history of its burning and the sort of conversation such meditation leads to.

~

Since our communal development schemes got no farther than idle campfire brainstorming that first summer, and the community itself died out even as an ideal early on, it is a reasonable question: of what use to us was our Coldstream property? The simple answer to that question is: recreational camping. For 35 years we have kept our Sierra property as a place to pitch our tents. Lacking investment, development, or construction ambitions, our business has been more or less the same as Thoreau at Walden or Hemingway in the good place of Big Two Hearted River. The idea, as always with pilgrimages, is simply getting oneself to the special place, partaking of its virtues and paying homage. The basic conversation, repeated over many years and many visits, is a litany of exclamations:

Wow, smell that air. Don't you just love the smell of pine needles baking in the sun?

Doesn't the water taste sweet? Doesn't it taste better when you scoop it up in your hands?

Isn't it wonderful to be able to look up to the ridge and see snow in the middle of summer?

Listen to those aspens (whose leaves, in "quaking," make a refreshing, almost tinkling sound in a breeze).

Look at the bleached trunks of those dead trees against the deep blue sky.

Isn't this just a great place?

Don't you feel good just being here?

This ongoing conversational appreciation has a little of the feel of running our fingers through our bag of coins: these natural wonders are ours, all ours . . . .

The first summer was our own little version of the Age of Exploration, an orgy of identifying and naming. Starting with our 20 acre rectangle and moving on to the adjacent territory, we investigated all the features shown on the topo map, tried all the trails, scrambled up every little unnamed, trailless promontory. We pored over the country like a sacred text.

Certain sites in the neighborhood became established over many years as special favorites. Less than an hour's hike up toward Mt. Lincoln there is an altar-like, large, flat boulder where, sitting crosslegged, you can get a fine, upclose view of the upper canyon and the main ridge itself through bluish air. Alternatively, stretch full length on the granite and surrender yourself to sun and sky; with eyes closed listen to the sound of air moving through the trees below.

Of course the big event of any visit to our land was the ascent of Tinker Knob itself, the highest thing around, a six mile, 3000 foot climb that takes some doing. The earliest years saw several climbs a summer but since then climbs have become few and far between. I believe there were more in the first two years than in the succeeding 30. Far more often in recent years the destination is the waterfall partway up the Tinker trail, just at the point where the climbing begins in earnest.

We take lunch to eat sitting on the rock beside the icy pool at the top of the fall.

~

My own most meaningful ritual over the years has been an early morning retreat on a certain whitish boulder partway up our property's western slope. I crawl stiffly forth from the tent into the grey chill of the hour, fill a small pack with water, a notebook and some reading, and trudge up there seeking the warmth of the first rays of the sun. I sit on my rock, do a little reading and writing of notes, letting the small sounds of the early hour seep in and erode my concentration, finally giving myself over to what can only be called communing with nature—that old-fashioned sounding term—in the romantic tradition of Wordsworth, Emerson and Thoreau. Communing with the nature of that place.

My experience of our place was very much that of one raised in the East. Somewhere in my early life —twenty years of cowboy movies were no doubt a factor—I got the idea that real mountains were all about deep blue skies, dry weather, snow-capped peaks and open slopes allowing for spacious viewing of them. If you didn't have all or most of these items, you didn't have real mountains. The only mountains that I knew before coming West were those of the East: notoriously buggy, damp, and claustrophobic, most of the bedrock muffled with topsoil, tamed by vegetation, the trees small and growing close together, spaces between them filled in with underbrush. Mountains were supposed to be crisp and cool and aloof; but eastern mountains were not remote enough or high enough to escape hazy, hot and humid weather.

My wife Susan and I packed into a lake in the Adirondaks near the source of the Hudson River one August many years ago. We had thought to escape the heat wave that was plaguing the cities, but in fact the weather in the mountains was in the 90s, the sky cloudless but grey with humidity and heat, rather like what we had left behind. We pitched our tent in the only available six-by-eight piece of ground amidst the jumble and congestion of standing and fallen and half-fallen trees and underbrush and sweltered and slapped bugs for two days, trying to convince ourselves we were better off in the mountains.

Heat wave in the mountains? A hideous contradiction in terms. But the Sierra, this "range of light," as John Muir, the Thoreau of the Sierra, called it, are as transcendent of such eastern phenomena as mugginess or pollution as Everest of the teeming, sweating subcontinent to the south.

In one sense this transcendent environment felt like the home this easterner never had in the east. In another sense I was always slightly amazed to be there, as if I really belonged to the other, messier world.

~

But the lower elevations have their uses. Arriving back from afternoon hikes we are often, even in the refreshing high Sierra, hot and dusty and tired. We like to think we can actually swim in the streams of our land and the daytime temperatures in the 80s make that a desirable thought, but the fact is the water, so recently snow, is shockingly cold, which makes less disappointing the other fact, that our deepest pools fall considerably short of what could legitimately be called swimming holes. Ceremonial immersion in the sacred waters is an appealing idea, but the fact is the typical Coldstream swim consists of a couple of spluttering strokes and a scramble for higher ground. Hence that spot on the South Yuba remained, even if an hour's drive away, a sort of extension of our Coldstream property. Tired of the grubbiness of a few days of camping in the dirt? You can always bail out: leave the tent, hop in the car and head over the pass for a few hours or day or two hit of the cleansing, relaxing waters of the Yuba. And it's not really leaving home: the headwaters of the Yuba originate in the high mountain valleys not far from Coldstream.

Bit Players

∧ ∧ ∧

We thought of ourselves as buying a piece of undeveloped nature—trees, meadows, streams—but we had
bought human history as well. Traipsing about our
acres and adjacent territory in the first summer or two,
we noted evidence that while our area might now lie
fallow, hosting nothing more important than our camping, it had been the scene in a previous era of more
purposeful activity, although often we were mystified as
to exactly what the purposes were. There was the debris
near the northeast corner that back that first summer
when I made my map had enough definition to warrant
the description "collapsed house"—who lived there?
how long go? and what were they up to? The gentle,
elongated hump you cross as you walk or drive into the

main camping area from Emigrant Trail is obviously a human earthwork, a mystery until I read about the dams used in ice making operations of olden times to contain winter and spring flooding and create an ice field. According to Joanne Meschery's history of Truckee, an ice industry flourished in our valley; in fact, ice from these parts "became known for its purity, considered so superior that in summer months it was packed with hay and shipped aboard insulated railroad cars to the grand hotels of New York City and New Orleans. There, guests beat the heat by sipping drinks frosted with crystal clear Sierra ice." It is possible that our property produced some of that well-connected ice.

Along the far bank of the bigger of our two streams, mostly concealed by bushes, there is a decaying structure that has yielded the redwood planks and rusty spikes out of which we have over the years constructed various items of camp furniture. According to Meschery there was by 1868 a booming lumber business in our area. To retrieve logs from more remote cutting sites, companies constructed V-shaped flumes, "harnessing the area's powerful water supply into manmade streams that carried logs swiftly to mills and railroad lines." To illustrate "swiftly" she quotes a W.F. Edwards writing in 1883: "The logs once at the top of the bluffs may be placed in chutes and glide speedily to the river. Speedily is not the word. They go like a thunderbolt. A stream of fire and smoke follow their flight, and they strike the water with a velocity which dashes the spray a hundred feet in the air." It seems likely that our redwood source was one of these lively contraptions, used to shoot logs down to the railroad, probably from what is now called on the topo map the Old Stanford Wood Camp. But what exactly was the wood used for, we wondered. Railroad ties? Fuel for the trains? Construction of the snowsheds used to keep avalanches off the tracks over the summit? And the redwood of the flume: was it really so superior to local species that it was worth importing all the way from the coast back before there were trucks? Or is the flume not as old as we have been thinking?

There are ruins of log cabins off the Tinker Knob trail most of the way to the waterfall, the massive logs still impressively intact, what's left of old doorways still recognizable as such. What practical purpose did they serve? Were they temporary homes for lumbermen in the old days? How did they manage to lift those monumental logs into place? When exactly did they abandon them, and why?

Thus our ruminations on the relics of a former era, our sphinxes, pyramids, Machu Picchu, our Roman aqueducts and temple ruins. They are from a time I am tempted to call the Heroic Period, but which could just as easily be called the exploitative era; in any case, the era of humans producing large, practical effects on raw nature, as contrasted with our passive, appreciative, absorptive relationship to the same territory. Our conjecture about the larger-than-life figures and goings-on of the last century reminds me a bit of the title characters of Tom Stoppard's play, *Rosenkrantz and Guildenstern Are Dead,* who are created wholly from their lines as minor characters in Shakespeare's *Hamlet.* They spend all their time trying to understand the story of which they are a part, but, like ants on a tennis court, are too marginal, too lacking in stature to appreciate the great drama unfolding.

~

We didn't have to guess about the dominant story of the area, that of the Donner Party, which we got in the version by George W. Stewart in his *Ordeal by Hunger.* The Donner party is for our part of the Sierra what the Mayflower Pilgrims are for southern, coastal New England. But it is much more recent history—226 years more recent, to be precise. Shakespeare was barely cool in his grave when his countrymen bumped into the New World; by 1846, when the Donner pilgrims were making their way to a still newer world, Thoreau, that proto-modern, was romancing nature at

Walden. While the famous story of the first Thanksgiving dinner feels fossilized as ritual and ancient history, the Donner story—also with a climax involving food— seems still alive in the undeveloped country of Coldstream. We hike the same, still unpaved roads they or their contemporaries pioneered. The trees along the roads are said to bear the scuff marks of their wagon wheels. Much more than contemporary southeastern New England, Coldstream seems haunted by the presence of its pilgrims.

The view from Donner Summit dramatically connects the viewer with the Donner story. Facing east from the summit or various scenic overlooks along Route 40 toward Donner Lake, you look down on a sort of museum of old roads, from the Interstate to the oldest wagon tracks, all preserved in the granite below. 40 itself, the two lane road which one winds up from the western end of Donner Lake is now closed in winter, which reminds us of the Donners' problem. I get a kick out of remembering that Route 40 was the only road into California through this part of the mountains when I first arrived in the summer of 1960, and that in those days the highway department was forced to do their best to keep it open through the winter. (Even its descendant, the vast swath of Interstate 80, closes in the worst storms.) It had been paved about twenty-five years when I used it to attain California, compared with the forty-odd years since then. Surveyed from the summit or an overlook, old Route 40 has more in common with the old wagon roads than with the superhighway which replaced it.

The Donner Party story is usually told as one of disaster and ill-fate, while the story of the Pilgrims, when it is recalled on Thanksgiving Day, is a success story, one of achieving a foothold in a new country. In fact, both groups lost about half their members during the first winter. We could, I suppose, just as reasonably choose to celebrate the half of the Donner Party that did finally make it over the mountains to California proper and, many of them, manage to build prosperous lives in the new land. And maybe we would, if the specific details of the ordeal they endured on the way did not make for a better story.

The difficulties of the Donner Party's trip from the Midwest across the great plains and mountains of the west are analogous to the Pilgrims' disease-ridden, cramped crossing of the ocean in the Mayflower. The Sierra, gateway to the promised land of California, functioned very much for the Donners as the continent's edge did for the Mayflower company. The problems for both parties derived from their tardiness. The Pilgrims first struck the tip of Cape Cod in November, sailed along the shore making occasional forays to land, engaging with the native population, and not until well into December did they finally commit to Plymouth as the site of their toehold in the New World. Anybody familiar with this area knows that December is no time to be arriving on shore without reservations at hotel and restaurant.

The Donner Party, when they arrived in Truckee, were close to their goal. They had only to cross the mountain pass a few miles away and then it would be all downhill to the fertile lands and mild, Pacific-influenced climate they had been told about; or so they thought. But back in Utah they had taken a shortcut that turned out badly and arrived in the Truckee area, from which they would launch themselves at the looming granite ridge of the Sierra, behind schedule, in late October. Even late October would not have been a problem in an ordinary year; but this particular year the winter storms had started earlier than usual. The pass, as their scouts discovered, was already clogged with three feet of snow. Another storm came in off the Pacific and they just never stopped coming all winter long, the snow accumulating to 13 feet even in the valley (as strikingly illustrated by the height of the base of the memorial statue near the entrance to Donner Memorial Park). They tried gamely to get over, which entailed winching wagons and oxen up the sheer cliffs, failed, returned to the eastern end of the lake and built crude cabins, which then got covered with snow. A small party of snowshoers set off to get help in the promised land beyond. Those who stayed behind eked out a grim, grubby existence under the snow, slowly starving. As the months went by they were reduced to eating their shoes, and then, reluctantly, as the most fascinating part of the story, started in on each other.

According to Stewart, most of the emigrants were appropriately reluctant and squeamish about it, weeping as they ate for their degraded state. One of the party, though, Lewis Keseberg, became infamous for his less than fastidious appetite. It was even alleged that he hastened a few of his fellow sufferers toward the inevitable (and eligibility as food), going to bed, for instance, with a weakened little boy who died overnight and was claimed by Keseburg, since his parents had no stomach for that source of meat. Afterwards, as one of the survivors—the best fed—he had the dubious taste to open in Sacramento, of all things, a restaurant. He actually bragged about his exploits and loudly recommended the taste of human flesh, particularly the liver.

The story of the Donners formed the ironic context for our recreational use of our property, as well as providing a source of wry merriment.

~

The other big story of the area was that of Charles Crocker and his Robber Baron cronies (including Leland Stanford, the founder of our very university) forcing the railroad through the mountains in 1868 in their race with other tycoons pushing from the East, eventually to meet up in Promontory, Utah, and be officially joined with the famous gold spike. Getting through the Sierra was the only really challenging part of the route and although the rich men tend to get all the glory, the real heroes were the thousands of Chinese laborers who actually did the work under the prodding of Crocker. It was they who, enduring the hardships and dangers of work with explosives, blasted and dug the holes through the mountain and notched the shelves in the granite that even today allow the trains to cling to the almost sheer slopes.

~

Winter was itself a formidable story to us fairweather campers. We would look at the benign meadows, the stream burbling obediently in its bed, and wonder: What's it like here, right here on our land, in January? The downhill skiers in our group knew something of the conditions confronting the members of the Donner Party. When it snows in the Sierra, it snows not inches, as in the East, but feet: the big, moisture-laden storms off the Pacific are often linked, making for days and days of almost continuous snow. At times the ski lifts actually run in troughs below the general level of the snow. The snow is so deep in many a winter that its removal requires a whole different kind of plow. You can't just push it off to one side, as with the plows that handle even the biggest eastern snowfalls. The Sierras have rotary plows that suck up the snow and shoot it through a tube overhead over the banks at the side. In a big winter, cars and trucks run in canyons of snow.

Stewart, in his *Donner Pass*, tells a story of Sierra winter that relates the saga of railroad to that of the Donners and brings both into the modern era. On January 13th, 1952, in a particularly big snowstorm, a train got bogged down in the mountains not far from our place.

> The plight of the 200 passengers and crew was not considered serious until afternoon when the only railroad rotary [plow] close at hand was overwhelmed by a snow slide and its engineer killed. Hope then rested in a single highway rotary, which had already been overworked and had suffered a breakdown. This rotary was some eight miles down the road, its crew

already worn down by round-the-clock work.
Because of the never-ceasing blizzard the rotary only fought its way through, heroically,
to make contact at eight o'clock on January
16, when matters were becoming critical on
the train. The stranded passengers and crew-
men were thus narrowly prevented from becoming another Donner Party.

This a mere sixteen years before our purchase of our
Coldstream property.

The skiers amongst us had experienced a version
of winter in the Sierra. Still, the resort context—the
grooming of the slopes, the society of other skiers—has
the effect of muffling the full impact. We were in any case
curious about what the other season would be like on our
piece of the Sierra. Seeking to satisfy this curiosity, in the
first or second year of ownership Harlan and I decided,
as a diversion from poor skiing conditions, to walk into
our property the five miles of unplowed road from the
gas stations that mark our interface with civilization.
Our investigation was fatally flawed in that it was only
a bit of January thaw that suggested the adventure and
of course skewed the findings. The snow was only a
couple of feet deep and compacted from recent rains.
We walked in, had our look around, saw that, at this
moment anyway, winter was not an entirely different

world from summer—our streams were not raging far and wide as we had imagined—and walked out again. We weren't fooled, of course. It was as if winter had contrived to keep its real face hidden from us.

~

Although hardly thinking of ourselves as in any real sense part of the history of the area, we almost immediatcly aftcr our purchase started having adventures of our own and began telling stories of them that soon enough achieved the status of myth, at least amongst ourselves.

One morning in the first year or two a girlfriend and I, abed in our tent, became aware of the drone of a plane overhead and suddenly of objects thudding to the ground around us. Emerging from the tent we discovered we were being bombed by chunks of 2x4 framing lumber, which, when we retrieved them, turned out to have a message penciled on them:

PICK ME UP AT THE TRUCKEE AIRPORT

Of course. Harlan's way of alerting us to a spontaneous visit. Perfect. What a great idea. Good old Harlan. We jump in the car and do as instructed.

Another story of the exuberance and high times of relative youth is an early climb of the mother mountain:

Harlan and I, accompanied by friend Jan's little dog Hoku, not only climbing Tinker but (so the story goes) taking it in stride, with barely a pause for the view from on high, then heading down the other side. On the far slope we come upon a large flock of grazing sheep and without hesitation, Hoku's sheepdog genes find appropriate employment for perhaps the first and only time in his life as he swoops down upon them, herding them joyfully this way and that in that high meadow. We stop by a mountain lake for lunch, throwing sticks for Hoku to retrieve, then in late afternoon discover ourselves in the vicinity of the ski runs of Squaw Valley, which we follow down to the Squaw lodge to our pre-arranged meeting with Jan and her car for transportation back to camp.

One of my favorite stories of Tinker is not of going up but coming down. Bounding down, as I prefer to tell it, for an appointment with friends at the Yuba, the usual hours of leg-jolting downhill trudge reduced to a half hour romp from top to bottom. I jump in my car, race out the dirt road, up and over the pass and on down the Pacific slope to Nevada City and the Yuba in the foothills, the Sierra a minor obstacle course, no match for my communal urgings. And then of course making it back up to Coldstream in time for the campfire dinner routine.

If that was the story of Youthful Exuberance Having Its Way with the mountain, there is another story about how the mountain almost had its way with me. My friend and brother-in-law Bob Pearson and I, no longer as young as we once were but young enough (at fifty) not to have much patience for our physical limits, decided that, having finally camped on top of Tinker Knob a few days before, we would strike out boldly, without benefit of trail, for the ridge between Tinker and Mt. Lincoln. It was only a vigorous half hour's hike up to high meadows right up under the ridge and from that point it seemed you could reach out and touch it. Why not just go for it directly, find a way up? Taking off from beyond the flat rock up the Mt. Lincoln road, we got into trouble dealing with the loose talus and crumbly cliffs up under the ridge trail. Bob scrabbled up between two walls of rock, yelled back down to me not to come, not a good route, and barely made it up to the Pacific Crest Trail. Meanwhile, having been advised not to go up, I began to feel very shaky about going down the loose stuff on the steep slope I was planted on. Finally, legs trembling uncontrollably, I made my way down a little and along the slope, a gentle traverse, got onto better footing, and met Bob on top some way down toward Mt. Lincoln. We were both very impressed with the amount of danger we had been in and arrived back in camp to tell the story of Two Old Guys Who Almost Bought It On the Mountain.

There was the time Sue and I, in a late spring visit, return from a hike to find the stream risen, from snow-melt during the warm day, and the corral of rocks in which we have left our cans of juice and beer cooling threatened by the flooding. In the process of bolstering the corral a few cans get loose in the current and we run downstream, with great hilarity, trying to head them off. I can't remember whether we got them all or any of them, but the whole point of the story is that we almost immediately began calling our frantic efforts the . . . Wild Juice Chase. The story quickly in the telling becomes less that of high, feisty waters in an earlier-than-usual camp than How a Great Pun was Born.

And then there is the story in which the downhill skiers among us hitch a ride on a westward bound train as it slows to a crawl around Horseshoe Bend, up and over Donner Pass, jump off near Sugar Bowl just over the pass, take the tram and lift to the top of Mt. Lincoln, and, to the confusion and admiration of regular skiers, point our skis down the back side, skiing several miles of unbroken snow back down to our property in the valley, ending up at our cabin, which we have had the foresight to stock with wine and canned goods. This one of course never actually happened. None of us were good enough skiers for one thing; the cabin never got built. We actually did, in our earliest enthusiasm for the possibilities of this place, brainstorm something like this; but once we had stood next to one of the trains as it went around the bend the idea was relegated forever to the category of Things It Would Be So Cool To Be Able To Say You Had Done. Maybe that's only twenty miles an hour the train is going around that curve, but upclose it's a massive twenty miles an hour and hopping one, especially with a pair of skis and boots in one arm, is hard to picture.

Thus some of the stories of the mock-heroic era of Coldstream Valley.

Short Arm of the Law

∧ ∧ ∧

Our legal ownership of that rectangle in Coldstream was the least important part of legally owning it. Or so I would have claimed, with a logic that made sense at the time. Nevertheless, one of the first things we did the first summer of ownership was to put up private property signs. Not, mind you, the usual mass-produced PRIVATE PROPERTY, KEEP OUT signs. We would never have wanted to be identified with such harshness, with the implication that the meaning to us of our piece of Coldstream had to do with either property or exclusivity, something we had and others didn't. With the agreement of the partners, using expertise gained from a part-time job a few years earlier painting signs for Stanford University, I got some redwood boards from the lumberyard and painted what seemed an appropriately gentle but firm assertion of our ownership:

ENTERING PRIVATE PROPERTY
PLEASE DO NOT CAMP
NEXT 1/8 MILE
COLDSTREAM MEADOW ASSOC.

I used yellow paint, hoping that the traditional National Forest colors would take on a bit of the endearing woodsiness and kindly authority of Smokey the Bear. This sign I nailed up on two roads as they crossed our borders, and another similar one at the access to our campground off the Emigrant Trail. All had been knocked down by the following summer, one smashed to smithereens. The attitude of those who shared our valley during the off-season toward the privacy of our property was clear enough.

Even as I manufactured the signs, I felt a little sheepish thus insisting on our ownership of just this little rectangle of woods, otherwise indistinguishable from the vast forest all around. I was sensitive to traditional local uses, such as hunting, far predating our johnny-come-lately purchase, and giving others perhaps a more natural, legitimate connection with our land than was conferred on us simply by putting some money down and signing some papers. On the other hand, I pictured this traditional off-season use as guys crashing around in our beloved woods, drinking beer and shooting up the place. Smashing private property signs.

The point of our signs was really not to make a big deal about the abstract, legal principle of our owner-ship. Mainly it was just to make it more likely that our established camping site would be available to us when we wanted to use it. Even for us self-styled purists there was something about camping on The Land that had to do with the ownership itself. We didn't want to camp just anywhere in the anonymous wilds; we wanted to camp on our own personal piece of it.

Every time I returned to Coldstream, nearing our part of the woods I wondered what would happen if we found strangers in possession of our traditional camping spot. And why wouldn't others camp there? To someone going along the road there were lots of inviting camping spots with creek frontage, and there-fore no particular need to camp on our land; but then our place would look to anyone else like just more meadows, creek and woods, just more National Forest. When we had been away for a couple of years, even we had trouble remembering just which woods along the road to plunge into to find our place. How would we handle it if we found others already encamped? At some point I began to arm myself with our deed and other documents with which I imagined myself establishing our rights, should the need arise (and used to fantasize their responding to my brandishing of paper by laughing in my face— and then what would I do?).

In September of 1973 I wrote a Mr. Toccalini of the Forest Service regarding our ownership: "This is to let you know that we do not want unauthorized people camping on our property, especially since those who did camp there this year left half-buried plastic sacks of junk, exposed beer cans, and built what we judge to be unsafe fireplaces. We will, in the future, give any authorized campers a letter signed by us. Anything you can do to keep our campsite, including some rough furniture we have built, from being harmed will be much appreciated." I have no idea what use, if any, Mr. T and his rangers made of my letter in going to bat for our rights.

I replaced one of the original, shattered redwood signs with a new assertion of ownership branded into an old board with wires shaped into letters and heated redhot in the campfire, hoping the handwrought mode of production and the use of local materials would prove more ingratiating than the governmental flavor of its predecessors. But it went the way of the others.

~

By a few years into our ownership, I had begun to get

the idea of how it is with private property that far from civilization. Suburbanite that I was, it had just never occurred to me before that there would be situations which would prevent full enjoyment of one's legally deeded property. But clearly the arm of Truckee law was not nearly long enough to provide routine patrolling of property five miles out Coldstream Valley that might rein in those hunters with their shoot-em-up notions of a good time; or, for that matter, any desperadoes who might want to use our land as an offseason hideout (we had seen those movies). If one were to make so bold as to build a house it would not be with the same sense of a man's home being his castle and all that I had been used to. I long assumed that if you built something, you would build it rough and sturdy and leave the door open, trying to win over with your hospitality those who otherwise would simply crash their way in. You might even appease them by stocking the place with canned goods. (Let them carry in their own beer, though, dammit).

In the '70s I used to wonder why the world wasn't knocking the door down to buy our beautiful property. Not that I wanted to sell this land which had been purchased not as an investment or commodity but for its intrinsic spiritual and communal possibilities. But I wondered why the few offers we did get were so low, no more than would be accounted for by inflation. At some point it began to dawn on me that what makes land appreciate in market value is the feasibility of building on it a securable house with the usual amenities. And since that is not possible on land with no available utilities, no roads in the winter and a bad road interrupted by railroad and streams in the best of times, and no effective police protection, it seemed likely any riches yielded by our property would go on being of the spiritual variety.

Unless, of course, the worst happened, and a big developer went in there and—dread thought—all at once brought the benefits of civilization to the whole area. In the early 1980s a story appeared in the newspaper:

DEVELOPERS PLAN SKI AREA TO BE
THE NATION'S LARGEST
Truckee—A group of California and Nevada developers is quietly planning what could be the nation's largest ski resort, a $1 billion complex in the Sierra Nevada. When finished, the proposed Sunstream ski area, nearly twice the size of Vail, Colo., would cater to 25,000 or more skiers a day. . . . The land, located in Coldstream Valley, southwest of Truckee . . .

As we became aware of the possibility of getting

developed into something even larger than Squaw Valley, the site of the 1960 Winter Olympics, located a few miles down the ridge from us, we did manage to assuage our grief at the threat to our solitude and the wild beauty of our land by guesses as to how much we would be offered for what, to judge by the arrangement of the base facilities at Squaw, would be the keystone plot in the proposed development, the land on which the main lodge and offices and bottoms of the lifts would be built. We wondered how much each of the ten of us would come out of it with, perhaps even including, as part of the deal, a ski cabin front row, center for each of us in this glamorous new resort.

But environmental concerns prevailed. A few years later we read:

HEWLETT BUY PUTS KIBOSH ON SKI RESORT

Truckee—Walter B. Hewlett of Palo Alto has bought 560 acres of scenic Sierra land near here to block development of a major ski resort. Hewlett, son of Silicon Valley pioneer William Hewlett, said he bought the land in Coldstream Canyon south of Donner Lake for about $650,000 . . . to preserve the land's forests and streams for future generations.

So we were not, afterall, to be faced with the dilemma of whether to sell our soulful acreage for a mess of pottage. For which, two hearty cheers.

Talk about ironic reversals. For Bay Area progressives in the '60s, the name Hewlett, as in Hewlett-Packard, had been synonymous with enemy of the people and all good things. In the spring of '68—we were already talking about the possibility of buying land—a few of the more politically active of the land partners were part of a contingent who occupied the Stanford student union building in one of the protests of the time. Packard was the fat cat Stanford trustee sent to talk us out of what we saw as our duty, paternalistically ruffling the hair of our leader as he made his pitch. And here, at least in the matter of protecting the people's land, a Hewlett— H-P money—ends up more on our side than we were.

Fast Forward

∧ ∧ ∧

The deepest current of this story is the pain of not being able to be all places at once. It belongs in the same category as the tragedy of not being able to have all women or eat all food. The tragedy, if that's how you live it, of limits. Of mortality. The very rich can afford numerous houses in glamorous locations—Cote d'Azur, Mustique, Vail; but they still have only one life to divide among those far-flung places. If they have much actual involvement as a citizen or community member in any one place there won't be much time and energy left over for anything but short visits to the others. The danger would be in not having much of a connection anywhere.

I have always, as it amuses my wife to remind me,

been one of those who want to live everywhere. Whenever I go to a new and attractive place—and there are a lot of attractive places—not content with sampling what it has to offer and then moving on, I find my way, even in a short visit of only a day or two, to a real estate office. When, stopping for gas along some desolate stretch of blue highway in remotest northwest Nevada, I interview the gas station attendant about rainfall totals and typical snow depths, I'm not just collecting information; I'm trying the place on for size.

Our Coldstream property seemed from the beginning to offer the possibility of having a real life of some sort in the Sierra. Part of the early experience was that, simply, of promise: the assumption that these times were just the beginning, that there would be deeper, richer times to come. Whether the formal community of friends worked out or not, my life would focus on this place. Occasional camping would lead to more solid lengths of time in more solid dwellings. In the throes of my infatuation I had the most honorable intentions. Mere legal ownership would turn into genuine commitment of some sort; promise would be consummated. And to an appreciable extent my life in other places has been distorted by that assumption and those intentions: skewed, stressed, thrown out of kilter like a planet whose orbit is disturbed by the gravitational pull of another planet.

What happened to all that promise? While I'm always true to Coldstream in my fashion, as the old song goes, here I am living (and writing this) 3000 miles away, as I have for many years. How did that come about? How, in the competition of places of the heart, did the east coast win out over the western mountains, the more domestic landscape over the wilder? The short answer is: it just didn't work out. You can't do everything. Best laid plans, and so on. Yes, but exactly how did it not work out? Just how did things turn out as they did?

~

OK, reviewing the years. The original communal impulse flourished all of one summer (if it can be truly said to have flourished at all except in my own mind). The summer of '69 was a Sierra version of John Denver's song about high times in a rival western mountain range. Most weekends the meadows were strewn with sleeping bags of friends and girlfriends and friends-of-friends. There was the exploring, the mapping of our land, the choosing of cabin sites. There was considerable partying around the campfire. It was indeed a high old time. There was the promise of more to come. I waited until the last possible minute to drive back East to resume my academic career, vowing to return as early as feasible the next summer.

And I did return. But it was not the same. Rather it was, but I was not. The summer of '70 following the spring of Cambodia, Kent State and campus shutdowns, turned out to be the watershed summer I more or less fell apart. I had spent the academic year teaching at Brown and living with a woman who had serious family ambitions for us. With the approach of summer, lured by the West's sexy freedom, I fled. With vague promises of renewal of our relationship on my return in the autumn, headed across country with a couple of friends in my old Volvo. But soon after my arrival in the promised land I was bushwhacked by dark psychic forces I hadn't known to be lurking inside myself, plunged into terror I learned to call panic attacks. Certain suddenly that my incapacity was some retribution for my unfaithfulness to the woman in my life, and that only she could restore my natural equanimity, within a week or so of driving 3000 grueling (if at the same time enjoyably adventurous) miles to get to the west coast I turned right around and flew back to ask her to marry me. She, seeing me clearly for the desperate and pathetic character I was, turned me down ("let's see how we're feeling in the fall") and I jumped on a plane and flew right back to California. That I would spend 300-some bucks of my $9500 assistant professor's salary in this mission still shocks me as a measure of the depth of my desperation.

Back in California, I was barely functional, the simplest conversation an ordeal of skating on thin ice. I clung to the closest friends, distracting myself from the panic with lessons in car maintenance from Harlan, seeing a shrink who kept me supplied with valium. Coldstream seemed a world for freer, less fearful spirits than mine. I had up to that point been a strong believer in the healing potential of certain good places—Walden Pond, John Denver's Rockies, John Muir's Yosemite. But in the summer of 1970 I discovered that Cold-stream was no panacea. In a letter written that fall I actually blamed the mountains "for being the object of my unrealistic dreams of community, for luring me away from the anchor of a good relationship."

Fast-forwarding now. . . .

Still under a cloud, but off the valium, in '71 I was back in California for the third summer since having moved back East, but only for a month, the one visit to Coldstream not with California companions but with a girlfriend visiting from the East. The summer of '72 for the first time I was not based in the San Francisco Bay Area at all but on The Land itself. After a short visit to Harlan I herded several young women, including a new girlfriend, up to the mountains to introduce them to the western pleasures of the Yuba and Coldstream.

Then in '73, for the first time since buying Coldstream, I didn't make it across the country at all. I
hung out with Phyllis in the then-shabby little city of
Providence, acquiring a taste for its desolate charms,
making do with nearby beaches. Finding that life was,
my prevailing theory to the contrary notwithstanding,
in fact liveable in the East without my fix of summer
in the West.

~

In the spring of 1974 my sister Polly was walking
along a Boston street when a car came up on the side-
walk and pinned her against a building. In part to provide a place for her to spend part of her long recupera-
tion and for other family members to rally round, my
sister Beeby and I decided to rent a house for three
weeks in Wellfleet, Cape Cod, Massachusetts. Wellfleet was not unknown to me. The fact is, an attraction
to this soulful east coast town predated my affair with
the California mountains by a number of years—I had
honeymooned here in my first marriage, in 1959—and
the three week vacation with family deepened my connection. A good long vacation with an assortment of
family and friends in Wellfleet emerged as a regular
feature of summer, a new pattern to replace the obligatory summer in the West. The Land lived on as poi-
gnant invitation—I'm not sure I ever actually planned

a summer without holding out the possibility of a visit to Coldstream—but in fact the East was sufficing.

The claims of life unfolding in the East kept me busy during the mid-'70s: making a move to a new job in another small New England city, Hartford, buying my first house there, then needing to spend a lot of time fixing it up; ending one serious relationship and starting another one. The romance with Coldstream yielded to the romance with Susan, my wife-to-be. The musty attic of an old house and the heat and humidity of a sultry August night—all so emphatically unlike California—provided the atmosphere of the first evening of this relationship that was to produce, at length, a child.

Yet another romance of place became a factor in the late '70s, a shared interest in tropical islands which absorbed some of our energy and time for travel and adventure. Our first vacation together was a couple of weeks in Key West, followed by more ambitious vacations in St.Vincent, a little-touristed island in the southern Caribbean, in Puerto Rico and an extended stay in Grenada, the year before Reagan invaded it.

~

By the time I finally made it out to Coldstream again in 1980, with Sue, eight years had passed. The visit had for me a quality of rediscovery. "Truckee is really bustling, much transformed," I note in a journal entry, "many of the storefronts done over just like so many other resorts these days—natural food stores, boutiques, backpacking stores, mini-malls . . ." Maybe we had not yet come up with the word gentrification for this sort of self-exploitation. "So many people, so much traffic downtown I was worried that The Land would be crowded. But in fact the old dirt road is just the same, very few folks down there. The whole place, in fact, seems wilder than ever. Really quite lovely and peaceful to be back."

We spend the first day just hanging out, rebuilding the broken down old picnic table by extracting rusty nails and pounding them in again—with a stone. It's mid-June, Sierra spring, and there's still snow in the shade of trees, making for handy campsite refrigeration. On a hike up the Tinker Knob trail to the waterfall we encounter solid snow at about 7000 feet, a wall of it three to five feet deep across the trail. We try hiking on it, but shoes get wet, the going is too hard, and we give up. Even below the snowline the trail is messy and raw, more stream bottom than trail in places. Isolated patches of snow are capped by dirt and debris. We have trouble getting across the swollen streams. At one point I tilt sideways, and the top of my daypack spills the binoculars, which go bouncing down the stream in

a foot or two of icy water. I clomp after them, pre-
cariously, in my high shoes. We explore, we cook, we
make love by the stream.

Thus Coldstream is reborn as an aspect of our relationship, no longer something, vaguely threatening to
Sue, that I used to do with other people back in some
golden age. Nevertheless, it was to be another five
years before we returned. That made the summer of '80
the only visit in 12 years. (This comes as a revelation
to me as I produce this account.) Houses intervened:
building new ones, working on old ones. Having abandoned my professorial career, I was finding it expedi-
ent to make myself into a carpenter and builder. By the
following summer I was heavily involved in designing
and building, on speculation, my first house, in northern Connecticut. Then, two years later Sue and I built
for ourselves a small cottage on a lot we had bought in
Wellfleet. In between the two projects we took a sort
of sabbatical and had planned to devote part of it to a
big swing around the West, including a leisurely stay
at The Land. But I began to get nervous about the abil-
ity of my old Volvo to hold together for the trip and we
never got any farther west than Rochester.

Building commitments kept my energy focused in
the East but in fact the impulse behind that first house,
if not the design of it, was a Coldstream impulse. A

couple of years before, before Sue had visited Cold-stream for the first time, she and I were driving some-where and I began to revive the old idea of building a place on the Sierra property. Wouldn't it be cool, I brainstormed out loud, not just to put up some sort of structure, but to spend the autumn and at least part of the winter in it? We would go out to The Land in the summer, set up camp, get a one room cabin built by the time of the first snow and then stay on, getting our-selves snowed in, with only the occasional snowshoe hike to Truckee for supplies. It was one part Thoreau, one part a re-enactment of the Donner Party, only, with the help of canned and freeze-dried goods (not to men-tion a supply of beer and wine), less ordeal by hunger and more actual party. I had not yet at this point built a house but the idea of building a cozy lovenest no bigger than was needed to keep the elements at bay, against a deadline of oncoming winter—Walden for two—seemed the ultimate building adventure and the ultimate wilderness adventure in one package. In fact there was a bit of a race against winter with that spec house a few years later, and the satisfaction of building a first fire in the woodstove of framing scraps while the season's first snow fell outside—but in the domesti-cated setting of a residential road in Connecticut rather than the Sierra.

The Wellfleet cottage was more in the small and efficient spirit of the original vision than the Connecticut house, but transplanting elements of that original Coldstream scenario to the Wellfleet woods made it that much more likely that of the two dream places, Wellfleet is the one that would actually be consummated.

~

When we did return to California in June of '85 the focus of the trip was not Coldstream but rather the wedding of Sue's brother in Palo Alto. There was, post-wedding, a general movement of Sue's family to the Sierra, but the visit did not live up to expectations. For one thing, the weather in early June still had a bit of winter left in it and it sleeted on our tent the first night.

The weather turned sunny but in memory the brilliantly lit Sierra scene is darkened by family events in the foreground: hurt feelings between Sue and her brother—I forget the precise squabble—sent Sue into self-exile to Truckee for a day and grew into a bitter separation that lasted more than a year. Still, the last note from the journal account: "Depressed descending into Hartford. I had left my heart in the mountains." The rest of the summer Sue and I spent getting our newly completed Wellfleet cottage ready to rent for income; and to get married ourselves.

A big part of the romance of summer in the West in the earliest Coldstream days was a temporal concept: the whole season stretching before one to the hazy horizon of fall and the resumption of the academic year; conceived this way summer was a small life unto itself. This visit of '85, the first in which we did not drive to and from California, completed the changeover to a much more limited, conventional visit, a week or two strictly hemmed in by scheduled flights.

However, in the inner tug-of-war between East and West, a new notion weighed in on the side of the West. In early summer of '86, on Martha's Vineyard, that bastion of summer life for northeasterners, including a large portion of my extended family, Sue and I had a breakfast meeting with my sister Beeby and her husband Bob about forming a long-term, communal plan focused on Nevada City, gateway to the Sierra. Not yet 50 but concerned not to leave our later life up to chance, we referred to this plan as a "later life community" to distinguish it from the typical American retirement scheme. Once again, almost twenty years after communal impulses had led to the purchase of The Land, Coldstream figured in discussion of a communal vision, although this time, it seemed, a vision that, based in established family relationships, stood a better chance of getting beyond the dreaming stage.

That visit to Martha's Vineyard was the same during which we announced that Sue was pregnant with Ben. The conversation about relocating to the Sierra foothills was energized in part by my need to believe that no rumor of a baby was going to deprive me of a future in my cherished landscape.

Not long after that conversation, with Sue four months pregnant, we flew out to Reno, rented a car and drove up to The Land. The defining event of this visit was what is now joked about (but not without a certain amount of real feeling that still lingers) as Brent Hounding Poor Pregnant Sue Up Tinker Knob. We did plan to climb and for the first time spend the night on top. I don't remember that I forced any part of this on Sue, although given her husband's fears about the pregnancy she would have been trying gamely to show that, with the right sort of spunky wife, there could indeed be Life During Pregnancy. The morning of our departure was fair, but by mid-afternoon the peak clouded up with what seemed like more than a local storm; we could hear distant thunder, perhaps a front blowing up from the south. It turned unusually chilly and windy. We went slowly, making numerous stops, Sue picking and identifying wild flowers; but despite the pace, she got very tired during the last, steep stretch. I was worried about the weather, because we had no tent and only Sue's poncho for protection (because, in my oft-expressed version of California, it doesn't rain in the summer). Yet I didn't want to turn back because I thought it would blow over and be gorgeous on top in the morning. But it was so miserable when we finally got there in late afternoon, with the hard, chill wind, and the threatening clouds, that, tired as we were, we decided to walk down and did it with only one break, getting back with daylight to spare. Sue was very sore and tired.

It turned out we guessed right in deciding to come down. Contrary to my theory of Sierra summer weather, it was so unsettled for a few days we chose to wait it out in Nevada City.

~

If the visit of '86 is mythologized as the one to show there is Life During Pregnancy, the summer of '87 was the visit to demonstrate that A Baby Need Not Slow One Down. For the third year in a row we returned, this time bearing Ben, now five months old, externally. We flew into Reno the last week in June, camped on The Land for a few days, drove to Nevada City to baptize Ben in the sacred Yuba flow and to meet up with Beeby and Bob, who were seeing all my old mountain places for the first time. They were liking it so much we were almost immediately looking for a house or land for our later-life family compound. At first I was gratified they shared my passion for the area I had for so many years urged them to visit. But then I felt bypassed by them, my place usurped by Bob, who, when I began to get cold feet, decided he would buy a certain house we had looked at in Nevada City with or without me. "They would end up with my California," I complained in my journal, "and I would be stranded in the East." I was relieved when the deal fell through.

We used our special kid-carrying backpack as a camp seat for Ben, perching him right up there in the fire circle with us. Not to be slowed down, I dutifully toted my son on group hikes, awarding myself points for parental virtue—as well as aerobic points for the extra weight carried. But there was tension between Sue and me. I would, following my old habit, crawl out of the tent at an early hour and make my way up to my ceremonial rock to warm myself in the first rays. No doubt, in addition to whatever other austere pleasures the rock used to serve, it now both symbolized and functioned as escape from the family tent. "On my rock up the hill," goes one journal note from that visit. "Tough night in the tent. Tangle of dreams, all of us awake some time in the night." Sue, carrying Ben, would locate me after a while and a certain sort of time would be over. There is a photo taken at the rock of Sue, babe in arms, looking grimly at the camera (and the photographer). I was put off by Sue's insisting on seeing our time in Coldstream in perspective, one vacation among many desirable options, saying things like "I wonder when we'll get here again." She wanted our next big trip to be to Europe. In the entertainment of such possibilities I saw betrayal of this most special place.

One morning it was cloudy—reality once again confounding the flawless weather of my inner Sierra—so we left camp early and spent much of the day at Tahoe. Escaping the stores, I took Ben and stood by the shore at the town beach taking in the scenery. But I was feeling trapped by the tourist scene, contrasting my lot with that of the participants in the Western States 100 mile endurance run from Squaw Valley over the mountains held that same day and only began to feel better when I did a bit of a run along the lake while Sue nursed Ben. We got into the campsite after dark, Ben screaming. Some of the traditional meaning of the Sierra for me was obviously proving to be immiscible with typical, unavoidable elements of family life.

~

What had started once again to become yearly pilgrimages to Coldstream continued in '88, this time with a solo visit. I rendezvoused in Reno with Beeby and Bob and their friends Gene and Nancy. This visit is most often characterized in our family as the time I abandoned my wife and young son in the East and slunk off disgracefully for a Sierra fix. (I swear I wouldn't come off much better if I had spent the entire time in the Reno sin parlors gambling away the family money.) It also happened to be the trip of the first and so far, in all these years, only overnight stay on Tinker Knob. There was wine with dinner in the shelter of a pine grove on the windy shoulder of the mountain, a restless but exciting night tentless under the stars, communing with distant vistas through sparkling air the next morning.

Returning to my life in the East, after an all-night, virtually sleepless flight, I descended into the inevitable heat wave haze, which always seemed an insult on returning from the bright, crisp Sierra, like deliberately lowering oneself into a vaguely poisonous netherworld.

But the Sierra renaissance of '86-'88 didn't stand a chance against the deepening claims of the East, especially our move fulltime to Wellfleet in 1992. Beeby and Bob made several trips West, pursuing a serious interest in buying land and retiring there, holding up their end of the retirement scenario, even if we were not. I lived my Sierra connection vicariously—and enviously—through their trips. Eventually, as it turned out, they joined us in Wellfleet as their semi-retirement home.

PART TWO

'96: Return to the Scene

∧ ∧ ∧

It was not until the summer of 1996, after another long hiatus, that we returned, Ben now aged nine, his father 58. I had become more or less reconciled to the idea that I might not have a future in the Sierra Nevada, that the history I had had there might be all the history I would have. But there we were again in Coldstream. Once again I walked the bounds, re-familiarizing myself with the shape of our rectangle in the wilderness. We took a number of hikes, longer and shorter, I moving more slowly and cautiously than in previous years, first from a troublesome knee I had been nursing for a few months, then from an ankle I sprained (in, of all places, the parking lot of the local Safeway). Because of this accident, we had to abort the big plan to conquer

Tinker and spend another night up there. When my ankle healed somewhat we hiked up the road and trail toward the mountain and located the waterfall. The log cabins along the trail were still standing, although noticeably settled and decayed compared with 10 and 15 years earlier. It occurred to me that although these old structures were ancient history to us when we first encountered them, our almost 30 years of appreciating them now constituted a significant portion of their whole history, possibly as much as 35-40 percent, breaking down somewhat the original sense of now and then, modern times and ancient history. Our own early hikes up this same path had become ancient history or would at least seem so to Ben, hearing me tell the old stories about them.

I found my way up the hillside and located my old rock for the usual reasons, to catch the day's first warmth and early morning quiet, one of the perks of being an early riser. Baby aspens that had grown up around it, and clambering up on top was a bit more of a project than it once had been. But the air smelled as sweet and new generations of chipmunks and birds sounded exactly like their ancestors, against the great background of stillness.

~

Approaching The Land after so many years away I

was prepared for disappointment. Surely the passage of time and the inevitable development and further crowding of that part of the world would finally affect the quality of life in Coldstream. Truckee, long since gentrified, seemed noticeably busier. North Tahoe, only ten miles away, was a trashier tourist scene than ever before and the Truckee River, which I had floated down in an inner tube in relative solitude over 20 years before, was now almost contiguous rafts rented from a number of concessions for 20 bucks-an-hour. But five miles down our dirt road things were gratifyingly the same, a peaceful pocket out of time.

Sitting on my rock I wrote: "Over the years and many visits, a theme of Coldstream has been how little it has changed, how slowly time seems to pass here. Here is one place at least, in this world of accelerating change, much of it development in the worst sense, where people have done virtually nothing to alter the scene. The most noticeable changes are non-manmade—erosion, growth—and those, even when viewed in widely spaced visits, are almost imperceptible. It's almost as if the sum total of all my stays, amounting all told to no more than a single summer season, is all the time that has passed since 1968, so slowly have things changed. Perhaps I find this sameness so satisfying because it creates the illusion that Coldstream really has no human life except for me—that it remains, despite my inconstant attendance, a faithful companion."

We had been told by Burt, the land partner who has looked after our interests over the years, that lumbering, that had seemed even three decades ago when we first came here to be long dormant, evidenced only in bleached, weathered stumps, had started up again. We had wondered what this renewed interest in our area would mean for our time there. We worried about the possibility of being violated by this violent business. Our ownership seemed a slight thing, a piece of paper in a file in some county office; why would it have any more effect on lumbering guys in their machines than it would on hunters accustomed (as we imagined it) to rampaging through the area every fall? And yet there was the large STOP sprayed with blue paint on stumps and rocks just short of our line, the lumber company's message to itself to respect our boundaries. We will never know how much their acknowledgement of our ownership owes to Burt's correspondence with them, to one of us reminding them of our existence. The corporate graffiti on trees just on and off our property was itself a discordant element, but otherwise we were left undisturbed by sight or sound of lumbering.

~

There was a moment, in the very beginning of our

ownership, when the nearness of something as big and loud and civilized as the railroad seemed a drawback, a detraction from our otherwise pristine setting. But soon the romance of the long freights with cars from many different companies and parts of the country, connecting these woods with the great world, began to make it seem an actual attraction. The railroad was a major feature of this visit because of Ben's obsession with all sorts of machines, the bigger the better; he had always been much more interested in the works of man than those of nature. Over the years we had left many a coin on the tracks to be flattened by trains, but never more than were squashed this time by Ben, for whom relating to the mass of those trains in this elemental way was big-time excitement. I was very glad for my computer-age son's exposure to this impressive pre-cyber relic of old-time America.

You can get a fine panorama of Tinker Knob and the whole spine of the Sierra from the elevated railroad bed of Horseshoe Bend, but we went there primarily to commune with the railroad itself, to walk the tracks, paying minute attention to mysterious notations on metal tags. We saw new ties, apparently replacements for the old ones, lying beside the tracks and wondered how they would accomplish the substitution. How would the railroad workers raise the rails and dislodge the old ties, which looked so solidly embedded, in order to slide in the new ties? And what was wrong with the old ones anyway? In the news at the time was a trip to Mars starring a toy car the scientists had devised to explore mysterious details of the surface of the planet 140,000 miles distant. And here we were having our troubles penetrating the mysteries of this railroad bed right beneath our noses here on earth.

We would be poking along the tracks heads down, involved in the minutiae, when we would feel or hear or otherwise sense the approach of a train, and it would unfailingly have the thrill of an advent, including some titillation at the danger of our present situation. (What if, in vacating the tracks, a foot got stuck, as in that movie, *Stand By Me*?) We would stand by the side of the tracks at a respectful distance, an American classic, exchanging waves with the engineers or the men in the caboose, watching the incredible weight of the cars actually depressing those tracks and ties which to us walking on them seemed so perfectly solid and immoveable. There is something undeniably exciting about witnessing this massive machinery thunder by. In one moment you are immersed in the stillness and solitude, in the next the quiet explodes in the furious passing of a train. And then the sound dies out, and solitude reigns again.

I had told Ben about the runs in the old days to see the train by night so one night after dinner when we heard the whistle he said: Let's go; and off we went. I found I was not as good at leaping to my feet with stomach full of dinner and running down a dark, bumpy road as I once was. (In the old days it felt like a short jaunt of a few hundred yards but it is actually close to three-quarters of a mile.) But I followed along and the experience of the Train at Night was worth the trouble, although I had the distinct feeling that, having passed this ritual along to Ben, I would feel less need to repeat it myself.

~

Drinking the sweet water directly from our streams, scooping it up in your hands whenever you feel like it, knowing it originated in the very snow of which you catch glimpses up under the ridge, had been one of the definitive joys of the place. In the first year or two I used to bottle it and take it back for use in the Bay Area instead of the processed stuff that came from the tap. (That water itself originated in the Sierra a couple of hundred miles to the south of us.). In '96, two sets of visitors to our camp raised the question of giardia pollution. Mark and Becky, Sue's brother and his wife, had equipped themselves with a water purifying device as well as pills. When I told of my positive experience over the years with the water, they raised the possibility that things had changed recently: more development, more campers. It is true we are hardly the wildest spot around, just five miles from a busy state park and a booming tourist town. But look, I said: there's the snow up there, here's the good tasting water flowing by, and no subdivisions or population explosion of campers—or bear, deer or cows for that matter—between there and here. And there are rapids; at some point I picked up the idea that water flowing as rapids over 100 feet of stones, being tossed into the air and sunlight, purifies itself. Why should I start worrying about the water?

But of course once the issue had been raised, I couldn't keep from wondering about all the concern over giardia. Apparently it had become just common sense these days to mistrust the water, no matter how wild the setting. Is there really more pollution to worry about nowadays, I wondered. Maybe it's been there all along, making just as many people sick one hundred years ago as now, but we've only now gotten around to doing something about it. Is that it? Or is it just an idea we have now: given the world population increase and the overdevelopment of nature, all the water has become suspect, even where it is actually less developed now than a century ago, as in Coldstream. Does our concern reflect an increase not in pollution itself so much as in the number of articles being written about it (a sort of information pollution)? Or had I just been lucky all these years?

I stopped at the Donner Park rangers' office to ask about their experiences. The first woman I spoke to, a young junior ranger, came up with the usual stern advice about not trusting local water lest one contract the dread giardia. The advice seemed more the obligatory story to be given out to visitors than water wisdom gleaned from actual experience camping in our valley. The boss ranger, on the other hand, confided that she had, personally, much the same understanding of the local water I had, could recall no reports of sickness from the water, had drunk Cold Creek water herself in areas where it had a good flow.

Later in our trip we drove over to the Siskyou Alps region of Northwest California, an area in general much more remote than ours, and I learned from the rangers of that area that it is well known that drinking water from certain creeks, even rushing creeks in high country, will give you intestinal diseases. The main reason given was cattle grazing near the stream even at high altitude.

~

Over the years there had been a certain amount of crude

construction, starting with arranging rocks for a fire circle and logs, steadied with rocks for sitting around the fire. Some of us for some reason, probably just for the hell of it, engineered a diversion of the stream closest to the campfire, damming a secondary stream and annexing to the camping area what had been a little island. We spent a couple of hours one time in an early visit at the farther creek trying to deepen the most likely candidate for a swimming hole by bolstering the existing dam—a tree trunk which had fallen across the current—with stones, sand, and old boards; we discovered that stopping the flow of a fast-running creek is not easy. We vowed that one day we would come with cement and do the job right, but as with other resolutions, it came to nothing. Harlan and I did in an early year craft a pretty nifty classic picnic table with attached benches of recycled wood from the flume.

All this activity, such as it was, was incidental, strictly ancillary to the main project, the enjoyment of the natural setting. A few days into the '96 visit the priorities shifted somewhat. What had hitherto been background became foreground. I had been sitting around nursing my sore ankle and moping about the collapse of our plan to climb and sleep on top of Tinker Knob. At some point I began to realize that I was dissatisfied not only because we had failed to accomplish the main goal of the trip, the big adventure in nature, but because we had not, in the first three days of camping, got the campsite organized. We had found no trace of the old picnic table and the campfire bench. The logs we used for benches around the fire were wobbly, the food a chaos of bags on the ground, leaning against the logs. Our kitchen was in disarray and we were too much on the ground

Something else was bothering me. The meadow seemed more loomed over by trees than before, a bit claustrophobic actually. The grove closest to the fire had become bushy with recent growth of pine, which made the traditional pantry (supplies hung from nails driven into tree trunks) useless and even made it hard to walk around the campfire. I had not recognized this before probably because the annoyance was masked by my nature romanticism: all power to eager, young growing things.

Out of this dissatisfaction with our chaotic campsite came a vision of development and improvement, which I sketched out for Sue for approval and modification. I would clear out all that pesky pine growth, get the grove back to the more useful shape it used to have. I would make us a kitchen counter, and some shelves. Civilization would once again assert itself here in Coldstream. We would get our asses up out of the dirt.

I started by cutting down what had, in my new perspective, become the offending new growth, except for certain two-to-three inch thick trunks I kept for supports for shelves. With some help from Ben, I limped over to the far creek to retrieve one more of those redwood planks from the old flume, now a third of a century older than when we liberated our first boards. In a break from the traditional romance of the indigenous, this time I brought in a supply of common nails from the hardware store to supplement the rusty, recycled spikes. I was prepared to go so far as to import a store-bought, contemporary pine board for a shelf, but it ended up not being necessary.

It was most satisfying engineering the main counter, supporting it at one end with a two inch trunk from one of the recent pines cut to the right length. A branch from one of the big, original pines that supported the other end served as a handy rack from which to hang pots and mugs. Opposite the counter, using eyeball leveling and other methods of spontaneous carpentry and camp engineering, I rigged a pantry of a couple of shelves. Part of that big redwood 2-by-12 nailed to a couple of the logs fireside became a sideboard. Finally, with one more, considerably more rotted redwood 2-by-12 and some legs cut from a three inch thick bleached pine trunk sticking up from the river bed, I built a small table for food preparation, a place to rest a glass of wine, and, after dinner, for playing cards.

All told, including the slaughter of the innocent young pines, the gathering of material from the farther stream, the designing and construction, this organizing work took no more than two to three hours and made a wonderful difference to camp morale.

So good was my feeling about these improvements that I became attached to them and could feel that I would not be entirely happy, on returning for the next visit, to find that my camp carpentry, the form I had bestowed on this raw setting, had become the raw material for some other camper's remodeling efforts—or worse, just fuel for an evening's fire. Probably the only real guarantee against that would be the design itself: my kitchen would prove so useful that no one would want to wreck it. But as an additional safeguard, before we left I made a sign, the first since the early '70s, I hoped would show that someone had taken the time to construct the present arrangement and cared about it. And that, of course—the appeal of last resort—it is private property, however reasonable the owners are about use by others.

PRIVATE CAMP: USE—RESPECT

I originally installed this on one of the log benches, but that seemed too intrusive, and perhaps, therefore, more likely to be rendered firewood, so I moved it to a pine tree in the adjacent grove, a demure distance back from the fire circle where it could be seen by those approaching (maybe encouraging them to look elsewhere for their campsite), but would not dominate their experience while there.

~

Since the three of us seemed to be having a good time, I felt encouraged to begin daydreaming once again about building that small cabin and spent some time reacquainting myself with the corner of the property, up the western slope, which I had long imagined as the site. When Mark and Becky visited, we talked about sharing the cost and work of erecting something, possibly in a somewhat longer visit the following summer. Perhaps Ben and I would go out early, right after school was out, meet Mark and get a headstart before Sue came out for a shorter stay.

Reviving the old idea of building a cabin was a logical extension of the camp improvement work, the fun and righteousness of being on The Land as a worker and builder, as opposed to just being there, period. How much of a jump is it, after all, from the improved campsite with counter and shelves and table to the same thing with a roof and walls? The idea would be, had always been, to make the cabin as simple as possible, especially since getting materials to the site and processing them once there would be such a problem. All one wanted was a more comfortable bed, a place to get away from bugs without having to crawl on hands and knees into a tent. Something a bit more interesting to put up than a tent.

One common contemporary idea about camping is that the proper way to respect the virtue and beauty of a wild place is to be there as lightly and unobtrusively as possible. The architecture most consistent with this purist's view of the wild, if you have to have a structure at all beyond the sleeping bag, which seems more like clothes than dwelling, is the minimal tent. My sister, the yoga teacher with mystical leanings, has more than once, as a lover of The Land, argued this position. "But we love it the way it is. Why would you want to go messing it up by building a cabin?" Less is more. To which I reply that a proper little cabin of the sort I have long fantasized, while certainly being no bigger than it has to be, would make the same sort of contribution to the beloved natural setting that Thoreau's cabin made to Walden Pond.

It was interesting to plan such a cabin, to figure out, for one thing, how much of the beloved scene to shut out. For instance, should it, after all these years of often rather pleasant experience with alfresco latrines, have a bathroom? My conclusion after 30 years of deliberation was: No, it should not. But just continuing the tradition of retiring behind bushes some distance from others probably wouldn't work either. The whole idea to that method is to move around to avoid running into your or others' old toilet paper before it biodegrades. Constantly searching for new spots might grow tiresome in anything but a few days' visit. (Having a cabin suggested longer visits.) A good compromise might be an old fashioned outhouse with a view, far enough from the cabin for privacy, close enough to be practical. I imagine in practice the precise distance would suggest itself, like the precise, although unconscious, calculation by which people of a certain culture stay a certain distance from others in conversation.

Sue and I discussed notions of living room. Would the modest little cabin need any place to sit and talk and read besides the dining table with dishes removed? Wouldn't the usual circle of couch and comfortable chairs lure one from the traditional campfire by the creek, a few hundred feet distant from the proposed cabin site, with its log couches and camp chairs? Should the cabin's living room consist of its own "outdoor room" in the form of a terrace with fire circle? But that would certainly set up competition with the traditional, communal fire. It would be too bad if the introduction of the more substantial housing technology put an end to the natural tendency of campers to come together at night for the shared comfort of a fire.

What about materials? Our neighbors, the Poulins, had taken the noble route and used only indigenous materials, logs and stone. How could we do other than follow their admirable example? On the other hand, it had taken them forever. The idea for our cabin had always included ease of construction consistent with lazy, protracted breakfasts around the campfire, hikes, trips to the Yuba, and other elements of vacation. Any more concerted effort would seem not to be in the spirit of the thing. Two weeks of part-time labor and 1000 bucks in materials is what I had always envisioned, no doubt optimistically. In that sense my light and quick cabin concept, in contrast with the Poulins' dense and labor intensive one, had a bit of the tent concept mixed in. But compared with a tent, with its alien materials—plastics, aluminum, synthetic fabrics—and wholly manufactured at a factory with no relation to our place, my cabin would use, if not indigenous materials, at least traditional ones such as wood and traditional building methods, and the manufacture would take place on the premises.

I assumed that some amount of pre-fabbing would be necessary; it seemed preferable to using a noisy generator to provide power for tools (and I couldn't really imagine making eight-foot cuts in sheets of plywood with a handsaw). I pictured myself striking an agreement with one of the gas stations out by the highway whereby for a small fee they would let me use their power and I would assemble parts of the cabin there. Of course that would require a substantial pickup or van; and what if the railroad crossing were not in? Plan B involved lugging framing lumber and 4-by-8 plywood sheets piece by piece the two-thirds of a mile from the railroad. This laborious modus operandi, contemplated, I must admit, only at considerable distance from the whole project, would put the two week completion time in grave jeopardy. It did have a certain attractive, meditative deliberateness.

I was aware that it was entirely likely this cabin would never get built. But it was enjoyable building it in conversation and sketching it in a notebook in some detail on the plane on the way back East.

~

Lacking a lockable kitchen, at some point in the '80's we came up with the idea of hiding essential camp gear on the premises. Friend Dick had made us a camp-warming present of a gigantic cast-iron frying pan that

weighed a ton and promised to make a most satisfying and useful anchor to our camp kitchen. Even the
purists among us had come to admit that chairs feel
better to aging bodies than logs or crude benches and
we had begun to import cheap plastic and aluminum
folding chairs, an indulgence that would at one time
have seemed an obscene violation and contradiction of
our whole reason for camping there. But we couldn't
imagine lugging the frying pan or bulky chairs back
and forth from the east coast on our visits, so we hit
upon the obvious, if primitive, plan of burying the
stuff. I found a place in the inner recesses of one of
our pine groves not far from the campfire site, dug a
shallow trench and covered the equipment over with
dirt, pine needles and branches. The only trouble is,
we neglected to note in which pine grove we buried it,
and where within the grove, so that the next time—a
year later? five?—we couldn't locate the site, despite a
considerable amount of time spent poking in the various pine groves. Somewhere there, underground, unless a stranger, or maybe a lucky family of beavers,
came upon our cache by accident, is a good start to a
hardware store. I don't think we ever got to use that
magnificent frying pan.

On the trip in '96, having searched once again in vain
for the underground camping equipment and bought

new chairs, pots and pans in discount and thrift stores in Truckee and Tahoe City, we once again buried it on breaking camp; but this time when we got home I put a note in the Coldstream file about how to find the stuff.

It remained a question: even if we actually did build a cabin, would we feel sufficiently protected as private property to store our *batterie de cuisine* there, or would we go on burying it? One change in our situation of which we became aware that summer was the expansion of Donner State Park into Coldstream. They had acquired most of the land between the prongs of the railway horseshoe, most of it a gift from the environmentally-conscious Hewlett, slayer of the ski resort, and intended to re-route the main access road through the park and control access. There would henceforth be a gate to which only owners would have the combination. I have not usually been a great rooter for civilization, but I found myself wondering hopefully whether, with Donner Park regulating things and a house newly built by the tracks, in addition to the Poulin cabin, maybe building a little place on our land might not be the risky venture it had always seemed.

Apocalypse Now and Then

∧ ∧ ∧

Either my latest sign struck just the right tone or, more likely, no one had set foot there in the intervening year. In any case when we returned to Coldstream the following summer we were happy to find the campsite exactly as we had left it, the kitchen remodeling intact. I was also relieved to find, with the help of the note I had made the summer before, the cooking utensils and tools (hammer, bow saw and some nails) we had stashed. We added to our camping amenities a big Revere fry pan, a colander and teapot bought in a Tahoe City thrift shop. The most satisfying acquisition was a gift from the railroad: one of the half-inch thick steel plates on which the rail itself sits. Ben and I copped it as a souvenir of our archeological investigations. The spikes fastening the plate to the tie were missing or loose enough to remove by hand; we trusted the one we took was not indispensable to the safe passing of the trains. It made an excellent griddle, holding the heat well, the spike holes allowing for grease drainage. We used it for frying the thin-sliced rounds of salami which passed for breakfast bacon. It pretty much superseded the previous summer's technology (of which we had actually been quite fond at the time): hot rocks overhanging the flames.

I had alerted Burt to our visit and he and Helen drove up to spend a day with us. It was, we all concluded, the first time we partners had met on The Land since the very earliest years, the early '70s. We were joined by Helen's daughter Cat, probably around 10 the last time I saw her, now so completely grown up there was simply no connecting the woman with the young girl, this present with that past. She seemed just another adult in the group. The obvious, visible changes in us all, child to woman, grownups to grownups-in-decline, were in striking contrast with the relatively unchanged setting. Our pace on a hike up to the waterfall was, shall we say, stately.

The major ambition of the trip was, once again, to spend the night atop Tinker Knob; we had even bought new backpacks for the assault. Once again we failed, this time because of threatening weather, including some three-eighths inch hail that fell for a brief period on the campsite. (Rumor had it that rain actually fell in the Bay Area, a meteorological event prohibited by law when I lived here in the 'sixties.)

So the big story of the visit was catching the logging company, in evidence but not actually heard the previous year, *flagrante delicto*. A day or two into our camping we were startled awake at something like 2 a.m. by the sound, of all things in this place where even a hiker going by in the middle of the day is a little startling, of a truck. It turned out to be a logging truck, the first of seven, each making three roundtrips a day up the Mt. Lincoln road to the relatively flat country up under the ridge, at around 8000 feet. There they would get loaded with logs, then wind tortuously down the same one-way road, with its loose sand and rocks—not secure footing even for hikers—and on out of our valley to a sawmill somewhere.

For several days, until they quit at what they said was the end of this session, this was a major fact of life. The morning after our rude wee hours awakening we hiked up the Mt. Lincoln road to check out the commotion that dominated the valley, emanating from on high. The road had been heavily impacted by the trucks, all the baby aspens along the way covered with dust. Up we climbed, following the ever greater uproar, past the big, flat rock which had always been the scene of peaceful communing with the close-up view of the ridge, to where the lumbermen made war on the trees. A huge yellow helicopter, of all incongruities, was manhandling huge segments of tree trunk three to four feet in diameter and 16 or more long, dangling them at the end of a long rope or chain, as if they were mere sticks, swinging them over the treetops from the less accessible area of cutting closer to the ridge to where the trucks were waiting to receive them. There was something obscene, on the edge of physically nauseating, about this, like the helicopter warfare scenes in the Vietnam war movie *Apocalypse Now*—this huge, roaring machine against all logic standing on the air, plucking giant trees like so many posies, lifting the forest, the very embodiment of stability and rootedness, into the air.

I was at first devastated by what seemed this terminal intrusion into our peaceful scene. But after a while, having gotten intimate with the operation, I felt somewhat less alienated from it. For one thing, I began to realize, it would not be accurate to think of this capitalist warfare on the forest as the Beginning of the End, the modern world finally doing in our precious valley. Coldstream was most likely logged clean 120 years ago; and now, every few years, there is relatively modest selective cutting. And as unwelcome as it is to be wakened by logging trucks in the dead of night, I am hardly an innocent victim of this lumbering. After all, I reflected, this operation or one like it is where the wood I use in building comes from. It was like discovering the headwaters of your favorite river: so, this is where our houses come from. Seeing this high country rapaciousness was at least more savory than a visit to a slaughterhouse, the source of the meat we eat.

I came away from this eye-opening visit to Coldstream wanting to get a book on the economics of logging that could explain how harvesting those trees can possibly be profitable, considering the probable cost of keeping that helicopter in the air hour after hour, the pilot probably pulling down big bucks to fly it, the chainsaw guys getting, one would hope, very good pay for their dangerous work, and whatever monetary reward it takes to get those truck drivers to start at two in the morning and negotiate those treacherous roads. And then after the mill gets the carcasses there is the cost of handling and milling and transporting them again before I get to see them at, say, two bucks for an eight foot two-by-four. I'm sure it all works out and the company gets a handsome profit; I just can't quite picture it.

One of the benefits of the logging was that for the first time in I don't know how long, the railroad crossing had been installed for the logging trucks. Moreover, a rugged bridge, completely unprecedented in our experience there, had been built to ease the trucks' way across the creek one otherwise must ford just short of the crossing on the way in.

~

More depressing than the logging business was the horde of 50 or so rallying motorcyclists who came down the logging road near our camp, their dust settling everywhere on and around us. Just good ol' boys, some in early middle age, out for a day of fun in the wild, heading for a destination, they explained proudly when we interviewed them, over the ridge and far away. They were skimming lightly over the country, obviously not becoming part of it even for a moment, buffered as they were from its stillness and pristineness by the dust and noise of their machinery and incidentally ruining it for all those along their route, at least for the hour or so it took them to pass through and their dust to settle. At least for the loggers it was a job. We headed for town in disgust.

~

Despite the troubling intrusions, Coldstream seemed more the old, peaceful place than not. I once again talked up the idea of a cottage and went up to the probable site to try on the views once again. We joked

about being all set up to start construction, what with
the SUV we had rented, the most substantial vehicle we
had ever brought there, the lumber company's bridge
and railroad crossing to facilitate the importation of
materials. But I felt farther from actually being in a
position to do this. Best bet seemed the idea of getting
out of Wellfleet for Ben's middle school, that dreaded
period, for a couple of years of home schooling in the
Truckee/Tahoe area, including the adventure of building
the Coldstream cabin as part of the learning—Thoreau
mixed with modern parenting. But I had my misgivings
about just uprooting ourselves like that from what has
become our home, even with the opportunity to realize
an old dream.

'02: Hoss and Ol' Bar Witness the End of an Era

∧ ∧ ∧

Two summers passed without a trip west; the Sierra were getting tough competition for the summer vacation slot from the south of France. In the autumn of 1999 I received an e-mail from Helen filling me in on further developments:

We couldn't drive across the railroad tracks so walked in and soon heard sounds of hammering and, egad, a table saw. Walked onto our land from the road and spotted the peak of a roof from 'next door' on the side with the road that fords the creek and goes up to the Tinker Knob trail. So we circled around and sure enough there was a man hammering away on a tiny cabin under construction and nearby was an identical cabin finished, lived in. We called out Hi and he came down off his ladder and introduced himself, offered some coffee. . . . They are a very warm, nice couple about 50 or late 40s, attractive. He's an outstanding carpenter/worker. Bought two and a half acres at 10,000 an acre. Got a permit to build. they live up there from snowmelt in the spring to water freezing in the winter. . . . He gets up early to get started working and she reads in bed up in their loft looking down on the beaver pond. It was enormously appealing. At first I was extremely displeased. Then, by the time we left, thought well, gee, it's kinda nice to have neighbors. They said come back soon. Made me green with envy for having all that time. I thought of you the whole time we were there, how you would go through the same thing I did about How Dare They, but how you'd end up liking them. And envying them.

So someone was finally doing it, making a real life in our place. In *our* place. I was glad it was Helen who happened to run into them, not I. It would be like meeting myself coming out of that cabin. There, but for the life I did lead, goes the life I didn't. The idea of fulltime neighbors, even nice ones, was upsetting. It's one thing being wakened in the middle of the night by lumber trucks; at least they are transients, here today making noise and raising dust, but gone tomorrow. Fulltime neighbors felt like a threat to the whole way things had been all these years. What it would be like camping in vacation mode when just downstream were neighbors living regular workaday lives in houses? Could I stand being reminded that they had done what I coulda, shoulda done?

So it was with curiosity mixed with trepidation that we returned in the first summer of the new millennium. We had heard that the neighbors had pioneered a new way across—or rather under—the railroad tracks. Following instructions, we drove down the road along the tracks and sure enough, it led through a tunnel constructed for the creek. I had more than once, following the creek, walked through that tunnel but it had never occurred to me that it might be a solution to the old problem of crossing the railroad. Our enterprising neighbors had, motivated by their more-than-recreational need, rearranged the stones so that a reasonably rugged vehicle could with care make it through. It opened up a whole new perspective: guaranteed access. No more arduous, unscheduled back packs into the land. Having neighbors clearly might have its advantages. Other than this welcome new route, we heard or saw no other signs of their existence that day. At camp, except for a large tree that had fallen across the usual way into our campsite, things were gratifyingly unchanged after three years' absence: the campsite was unoccupied by alien campers, camp furniture still intact, the buried kitchen stuff discovered where I had stashed it. Our land was pristine, peaceful, almost as if waiting for us.

Next morning we took an exploratory walk along the road back toward the tracks and up the road to Tinker and sure enough, as foretold by Helen's e-mail, there were our new neighbors, Kathy and David Robertson, producing civilization on a scale the valley had not seen for over 100 years, if ever. Helen's description had prepared me for a sort of married couple version of Thoreau and his tiny cabin in the woods. But by the time we arrived not only had the two cabins she had mentioned been finished, the neighbors were well into construction of a large, lodge-like structure out of local wood and stone. An impressive arsenal of heavy earth -moving machinery, all apparently owned by the neighbors, stood about here and there in the dusty job site. These people were serious. They were also very friendly and took us on a tour of their various projects, including a rooftop photovoltaic array; they were determined to have their comforts but the grid was still five miles away.

That evening we drank wine sitting in real furniture overlooking our neighbors' beaver pond with beavers sporting in it. We had always assumed that while beavers had once been busy on our place—there were gnawed tree trunks all over our land—they had migrated elsewhere. And yet here was a pond full of them just a few hundred yards downstream from us.

In addition to beavers, the neighbors said they had seen bears and coyotes. One of the features of our camping experience in Coldstream over the previous 30 years had been the almost complete lack of animals larger than birds and squirrels. Yosemite was famous for its pesky bears; we wondered, while being grateful we didn't have to deal with them, where our bears were keeping themselves. We had, in the early years, heard coyotes yipping from far-off. It made us easterners, whose West had been largely a cinematic experience, feel like cowpokes or desperadoes a-settin' around the campfire in the old westerns. But I had never actually seen a coyote until in the early '90s they somehow (and for reasons of their own) showed up here on Cape Cod, where they were becoming as common as other domestic wildlife such as possums, skunks and raccoons. (I must say I found this intrusion of the imagery of the wild West into the tame East as aesthetically displeasing as a badly mixed metaphor.) Meanwhile in the wild West, I hadn't even heard one howl for a long time. But here were the neighbors talking about coyote and bear sightings as if they were common occurrences. It seemed that in a couple of years our place had yielded up more secrets to these newcomers than to us owner-tourists in the previous three decades. As if to illustrate the Robertsons' version of wildlife reality, I saw a coyote myself when jogging down the dirt road, my first one in all those years.

Sitting in the dark hearing the stories about large animals it was reassuring to have the nearby company of buildings; one imagined the bears being impressed with this substantial establishment and giving it a wide berth. Essentially the same activity upstream at our place seemed a whole different thing. Sitting around a bit of flame surrounded by dark wilderness with only one's voice and maybe some wine for reassurance made one feel considerably more vulnerable. On leaving we reciprocated the neighbors' hospitality, inviting them to come up and have a drink at our place, but I was thinking: would they really leave all this splendor to come sit at our lowly campsite? Perhaps they would welcome the opportunity to get back to basics.

Having seen the beavers with our own eyes, we for the first time gave in to the general concern over giardia in the water. If there were beavers just downstream from us, there could be beavers upstream. We began after 30 years importing water, which, although a considerable defeat and an insult to the natural product flowing in our creek, turned out to have its compensations. The alien water came in five gallon plastic containers which could conveniently be set up on a table and accessed through a handy spigot.

We happened to mention to the Robertsons the fallen tree that blocked the usual access to our campsite and returned the next day from a long hike to find that David had brought one of his several large chainsaws over and cut a section out for us to drive through. This heroic intervention was a mixed blessing. Sue, Ben and I had decided after some discussion of ways within our means of getting around the obstacle, that, after all, convenience wasn't everything and we rather liked keeping the car at a couple of hundred feet distance. But of course once the way was cleared by the neighborly act we drove right through and convenience won the day, as it usually does if available.

Our neighbors told us when we were drinking wine and observing beavers that they had some thought of establishing a business, maybe some kind of inn, taking advantage of being at the gateway to Tinker, as it were, the last bit of civilization before you head up toward the top, and the first you hit, dusty, hungry, thirsty, on the way down. In fact that very evening some women straggled in at the end of a hike up the mountain lost and scared and the Robertsons were able to give them reassurances and directions. Maybe if they had been open for business they would have been happy to rent a room for the night. Something about our neighbors' situation reminded me of a western movie. For a couple of days I couldn't put my finger on just which movie, but then it came to me: *The Ballad of Cable Hogue.* Over 100 years later, but the same scenario: our neighbors were constructing a contemporary version of the store Cable Hogue (Jason Robards) builds in the movie, crazily enough it seems at first, out in the middle of nowhere on a trail leading to a tiny frontier town. His foresight is rewarded when the town grows, making him a powerful and wealthy man. It was still mostly wild out there in Coldstream-beyond-the-tracks, but who knows what our neighbors might be in the middle of some day?

Inspired a bit by the neighbors' industry, I located one more of those 2-by-12s from the sluice (surely this time the last) and made a picnic table. Not as fancy as the one we built 30 years before with its integral benches, but a nice improvement to our camp nevertheless. That night we ate at it with our new folding camp chairs; later in the evening Ben and Sue played cards at it.

Camping actually went more or less as it usually did. But if the neighbors were Cable Hogue, we felt a little like—Daniel Boone was it?—the frontiersman who said something about knowing it was time to move on when he could hear the sound of his neighbor's rifle. For us it was the sound of the neighbor's backhoe—not so much the sound actually—the sporadic construction noises from down the creek, like the chattering of birds and chipmunks, really didn't make much of a dent in the general stillness. And yet the knowledge that they were there, doing what they were doing, changed everything.

~

Bob Pearson and I returned in September of 2002, braving rumors of bubonic plague, of all things, which we might have taken as an omen, if we had been of a superstitious bent. (We were assured by Donner Park rangers, that although they were taking the problem seriously enough to have closed the park over Labor Day and indefinitely after that, if we stayed away from any rodent corpses we found lying around we shouldn't have any problem.) We found the Robertsons driving hard to finish their main building; once again they graciously made time to show us around. Especially striking was the central fireplace of massive peeled local tree trunks and huge boulders. How did you put these things in place, we asked? and heard the story of how they brought in a crane on the railroad over Donner Pass and then on other conveyance, up the slope at Eder, over one of the old pioneer routes, a monumental undertaking, worthy of the old days of carving tunnels through the mountains, winching oxen over passes.

Getting down to the business of camping, we discovered evidence that others had camped there in our absence, but the evidence was all positive. As part of our campaign in 2000 to welcome campers and encourage respect for our site, Ben had nailed to a tree a plastic Ziploc bag containing a small notebook inviting remarks. Bob and I found this, somewhat the worse for having weathered two winters, containing several enthusiastic comments. Even more heartening, not only had our campers not seen fit to use our existing furniture for firewood, someone had actually contributed several dark green, hard plastic chairs to the stock of camp furniture, a most welcome addition.

Sometime in the middle of the first night or two I woke hearing sounds of an animal apparently getting into our food. One of the very pleasant things about camping on our land had always been the complete lack of nighttime marauders. In Yosemite, when we camped there in the early '80s, Sue and I were seriously warned that to protect your food from bears you had to find a tree with a long branch 30 feet off the ground, suspend your food in a bag from the very end of that branch; or alternatively, midway on a rope stretched between two trees at the same height, both of which methods would seem to require extension ladders. But in Coldstream, beyond the minor nibblings and pilferings of an enterprising early bird or chipmunk we had never had the problem. Most evenings before retiring we just tidied up but took no care to put our food away. But there I was lying rigid and alert in my sleeping bag wondering if what I was hearing was a bear finally taking an interest in us, and if so, would it, once it had had its way with our food supplies, start investigating the contents of my tent? Finally, curiosity overcoming fear of the unknown, I unzipped one corner of the tent door, stuck my head out and pointed the flashlight in the direction of the noise: shining eyes; raccoon. Considerable relief. But still, a wild animal, and a bold one. It did not immediately withdraw once my beam had discovered it. Even when I crawled out and stood up to display the full size and majesty of our species, it didn't seem properly impressed and only reluctantly gave ground, sidling toward the dry stream bed. Later the same night it returned. After that we made it a practice to secure everything in the SUV, realizing that not very often in the history of our camping would we have had the luxury of that solution.

The very morning after the incident with the raccoon I came back from an early morning ramble to find Bob himself secured in the SUV. He had been doing campfire chores when our neighbors' large dog, to whom we had been introduced but with whom we were not yet on a first name basis, approached in what Bob interpreted as a menacing fashion from across the creek. Bob thought it prudent to abandon the field to him and retreated to the SUV to await further developments. By the time I arrived the dog was gone, I reassured him, and we re-took possession of our camp.

Raccoon, big dog? Both unprecedented in 30 years. What was going on here?

Later we made a point of stopping by the Robertsons to register a friendly complaint about the dog and were told, with sympathy, that they had gotten him to keep off the bears that had begun to come around. And yes, apparently the dog was not sufficiently clear on the job description to discriminate between bears and people. We were not the only ones to have been frightened by him. They had him on some kind of electronic leash, but it had broken. Wouldn't happen again.

Over the years almost all of our visitors were imports,

old friends who had been alerted that we would be at home in the Sierras and who kindly drove up from Bay Area to visit in this place which seemed to enhance such reunions. This year was no exception. Dick and Sue came and we spent an afternoon drinking wine and exchanging photos and stories of our recent lives. Burt came up with a new romance and spent the night. Mark Weegar came up for the express purpose of pushing us old guys up Tinker for the first climb in over 15 years. But this was the first time in which such imported socializing had competition from local visitation. We had the first visit from Art Poulin in many years and we passed a pleasant hour or two around the fire with him drinking wine and waxing nostalgic about the earlier years in our three decades of acquaintance (even if it has been only about three hours of actual face time over all those years) and hearing stories about contemporary life in the valley. Next morning, sitting around the campfire waiting for the sun to get up above the trees across the creek and warm us, we were hailed from across the meadow and then joined by Maggie, an outdoorsy-seeming woman apparently in her 30s, who said she just came by to be neighborly, had a part-time residence, a trailer, down near the tracks. She mentioned having several neighbors down that way.

Maggie invited us to visit, so on our last full day

of camping, returning from a jog in that direction, I stopped to find her place and wound up talking to yet another neighbor, a friendly guy in his 40s named Mike. Formerly of Truckee, he was now living in Sacramento but got up to Coldstream as often as he could. It was in this conversation, standing in front of Mike's banged-up trailer, that I first learned that a neighborhood association of sorts had begun to meet to discuss the possibility of a more legitimate way under the tracks than the Mouse Hole, as the tunnel under the tracks is now familiarly known. The railroad, worried about liability, had threatened to close it down; in any case, although a huge improvement over having to pack your stuff in, it is far from ideal, hard on the undersides of vehicles and involving an inconvenient detour down one side of the tracks and back up the other side to the main road. (Mike said the dents and scrapes in his trailer were a result of the tight squeeze through the Mouse Hole.) The logical thing, since the Emigrant Trail, the dirt road out from civilization back through our properties is, however poorly maintained, a legal public way, why shouldn't it be improved with a tunnel of its own under the tracks? That was not entirely a rhetorical question; some owners had raised the issue of whether convenience and ease truly constitute an improvement. But meetings were being held, Donner State Park was in on the negotiations; it seemed that the idea was taking hold and might in time be realized.

As I walked the half mile from Mike's trailer back to our camp processing this new information, putting it together with what I had gleaned from visits with the Robertsons, Maggie and Art, it began to sink in that our end of Coldstream Valley was in the process of radical change. While we weren't looking we had become a neighborhood, what they would have called a settlement in the old days. The Robertsons, the Cable Hogues of Coldstream only two years before, suddenly seemed not so much an outpost as part of the nucleus of a Coldstream-Beyond-the-Tracks village.

And where, exactly, did that leave us oldtimer owner/campers? Camping in a neighborhood, as we were discovering, had certain problems. For one thing, it seemed entirely plausible that our new neighbors had not been seeing more wildlife because, spending more time here they were more tuned-in; on the contrary, with the exception of the beavers, which had probably been living down the stream on their property all along, they were seeing more wildlife because they were themselves attracting the wildlife. For the first time in our era human activity, theirs and other neighbors', was providing something—garbage mainly—to interest bears, coyotes, raccoons. (You know things are getting too civilized when the wildlife arrives.) The wild animals had come for the garbage; and the big dog of dubious disposition had been imported to deal with the wild animals. Our first-time-ever encounters at the campsite were most likely part of a new pattern. Beyond these inconveniences, it just feels different to be sleeping on the hard ground under a cloth roof, when neighbors are sleeping in a soft bed under a hard roof. (Full disclosure: as a concession to the aging body, I had come prepared with a $49.95 inflatable double-size mattress which filled most of the floor space of my venerable tent. It was better than the old, slippery Thermarest but fell well short of an actual bed.)

There's a children's story which starts with a little house on a country road. A nearby city expands until the little house is completely surrounded by skyscrapers. (I think there may be something about the owner refusing to sell out to developers). I remember a picture of the little house looking anxiously up at the buildings looming over it. That story catches just a bit of what it had begun to feel like to live in a tent in the new Coldstream.

And if it felt that way now, how would it be when the new underpass went in? That might still be years off, but the meaning of it began immediately to affect our feelings about the place. Accessibility would no longer be a deterrent to development. How long before we were tenting amongst condos? And even if I were finally to get my act together and build that cabin, the long fantasized project would have an entirely different meaning: not our version of what the Poulins had built in the '70s, Thoreau in the mountains, but part of a woodsy suburb of second-homes.

On the Tinker climb Bob and I had given ourselves western trail names. He was Hoss, I was Ol' Bar. It was part of the joking camaraderie of the trail; but given the changes in Coldstream, there was a serious level to it. On a side trip to Nevada City I had picked up in a thrift store, against the chill of the longer nights of our early autumn camping, a long, dark coat. The very coat, I was convinced, Clint Eastwood wore in *High Plains Drifter*. I replaced my usual shapeless, cloth cap with a wide brimmed, leather hat. It was a fedora actually, but in my self-image I westernized it into the more serious, macho headgear Clint wore with that long, dark coat. Something about that outfit felt comforting in this new situation. Hoss and I felt like throwbacks, like the retired Texas Rangers in *Lonesome Dove* who come into a town they had years before helped to get started and realize that their time is over, that history has left them behind.

"Hoss," said Ol' Bar, when he got back to camp that

morning, "I been thinkin'. I believe that right here and now on this here trip we are witnessing the end of the era of roughing it here in Coldstream. Leastways, no more camping here for Ol' Bar. Either I figger out how to get that cabin built or I ain't comin' back."

I had made vague threats of this sort before in trying to enlist sympathy for the idea of a cabin; but this time I meant it.

Epilog

^ ^ ^

It's been a couple of years since that last visit with Hoss (who has kept his western trail moniker on our regular lunches and golf dates). I haven't been back, although The Land is never for long out of my mind. Funny thing. Over the course of over three decades of owning in Coldstream Canyon, in the months and years between infrequent visits, my connection with the place consisted solely of memories, images, flash-backs—and lots of yearning on my part—but no actual information. Most of the time Coldstream was more mythical than real. Now, since 2002, I've been in e-mail connection with one neighbor, Mike of the dented trailer, who has kept me up to date on the underpass committee, of which he happens to be the chairman.

And after about two hour's worth of actual face time over all the years of sharing a long boundary, Art Poulin and I have been chatting regularly online. A Californian, he visits his cabin in Coldstream regularly in season and sends me dispatches.

I made it into the tracks last weekend. Stopped on way in to "rescue" a sad looking woman with a tiny dog on a leash walking out. She looked so weary I had to turn around and drive her out to the gate. I think her lack of front teeth caused her to slur her words. She claimed she had been abandoned back up the road somewhere. Couldn't get much other info from her. I hoped she hadn't invaded the cabin. When asked if there was any snow on the road farther in she said no. She mustn't have been on our side of the tracks. There were large patches of snow along the road there.

Emigrant Creek was low enough to drive through to get close to the tracks. Cold Creek was a raging torrent. Broke down the Dave & Beaver dam as well as torqued Dave's bridge. My meadow looked like a lake. Several ducks enjoyed it. Weather was great, scenery spectacular, enjoyed three days of solitude. Plan to return with wife and dog this week.

I'm back home after a failed venture up to Coldstream. Dave had reported 8" of snow on our side of the tracks and a scraped road from gate to tracks. He was right, but he failed to mention that no one had driven down our section of the road after the Forest Service sign. I had been in 4WD since the mouse hole but that didn't help when the road was blocked by a beaver-weakened aspen. Luckily I had a chain saw with me and dispatched the tree, adding some logs to the side of the road. I must have hit some 8 1/2" snow when I got to my place because my truck slipped to one side and I was bogged down. After plenty of shoveling and maneuvering I was able to point the truck toward the tracks ready for an escape in case of a sudden snow fall. Then I discovered that my tail gate was broken and wouldn't open. This made it less than fun trying to lift my ailing dog out of the truck.

After hauling my junk up the hill to the cabin it was dark and cold—30 degrees at 7:00

*p.m. A fire in the stove, a dinner, a couple of
chapters of a book and I crashed. This a.m. I
heard on the only station our radio receives
that there was a storm warning for our area.
Not being macho enough to ignore it, I set
about closing up for the winter. This took me
most of the day. When I pulled out the clouds
had come in. I was bundled up in three lay-
ers of clothes as we pulled out. After going
through the mouse hole and stopping to un-
lock the front wheel hubs, I was surprised to
see another vehicle approaching. The driver's
window was open and Maggie Graff stuck her
arm out and waved. She was wearing a short-
sleeved shirt. Ah, youth! I'm home and feeling
I was a wimp for not staying.*

"Home" for Art is Cazedero near the northern California coast, a completely different sort of environment,
and that's where he probably does his e-mailing, but
here at my computer on the other side of the country
I'm picturing him in Coldstream and getting my vicari-
ous hit of our place.

Thus the nature of the contemporary relationship
to places. Now that I've decided that I'm done with
Coldstream (unless we build that cabin), I'm more

intimate with it than ever before, thanks to e-mail. What they mean by Information Age, I guess. Weird. I'm expecting to receive a cell phone call from the top of Tinker Knob any time now, putting me up there (like the call the guy in Krakauer's *Into Thin Air* made to his wife in Australia while he lay freezing to death at the summit of Everest.)

~

It occurs to me that as the cabin possibility seems more and more remote, selling begins to make sense. Our twenty acres are not doing us any good just sitting there. How would we go about selling? Could we even manage to round up the old partners, with several of whom others of us have had no contact or word of in all these years? Presumably they would have no objection to selling. On the other hand, Ben, now 17 and tooling around in his first car, has been talking recently about how awesome it would be to drive across country the summer after high school with a couple of friends and build a little cabin on our land in the Sierra. I love the thought of him having some future on that land.

Thanks . . .

. . . to old friends Bob Pearson, Stuart Alpert, and Stephan Michelson, all of whom read this in various stages and made useful comments that influenced the final product.

About the Author

A former English professor and recovering romantic, Brent Harold has for 12 years written an op-ed column for the Cape Cod Times. He is the author of *The Novel and Human Problems* and, recently, of *Wellfleet and the World: Themes of a Cherished and Threatened Place.* He lives with his wife and son in Wellfleet, Massachusetts on outer Cape Cod.

ABOUT THE TYPE

This book was set in Times, a modernized version of the older typeface, Plantin. It was commissioned and created in 1931 for *The Times of London* for use in the body copy of the paper. The design process was supervised by Stanley Morison. The Times font subsequently became the workhorse of the publishing industry and continues to be very popular